My First Dictionary

Written by
Betty Root

Illustrated by
**Mark Ruffle, Jenny Snape,
and Jonathan Langley**

DK Publishing

DK

London, New York, Melbourne, Munich, and Delhi

DK UK
Senior Editor Dawn Sirett
Project Art Editor Victoria Palastanga
U.S. Editor Jennifer Quasha
Category Publisher Sue Leonard
Design Development Manager Helen Senior
Publishing Director Mary-Clare Jerram
Production Editor Marc Staples
Production Controller Jen Lockwood

DK India
Editor Nidhilekha Mathur
Art Editor Nitu Singh
Assistant Art Editors Vikas Sachdeva, Rohit Walia
DTP Designers Anurag Trivedi,
Arjinder Singh, Arvind Kumar
Picture Researcher Sakshi Saluja
Managing Editor Glenda Fernandes
Managing Art Editor Navidita Thapa
CTS Manager Sunil Sharma

First American edition, 1993
This revised edition, 2012

Published in the United States by DK Publishing
375 Hudson Street, New York, New York 10014

12 13 14 15 16   10 9 8 7 6 5 4 3 2 1
001–183881–Aug/2012

Copyright © 1993, 2012 Dorling Kindersley Limited
All rights reserved

Published in Great Britain by Dorling Kindersley Limited.

A catalog record for this book is available from the Library of Congress.

ISBN 978-0-7566-9313-8

DK books are available at special discounts when purchased in bulk
for sales promotions, premiums, fund-raising, or educational use.
For details, contact: DK Publishing Special Markets, 375 Hudson Street,
New York, New York 10014 or SpecialSales@dk.com

Printed and bound in China by Hung Hing

Discover more at
www.dk.com

Contents

Notes for parents and teachers   3

Dictionary word entries   4

Dictionary games   92

Index of additional words   96

Notes for parents and teachers

My First Dictionary is a colorful introduction to the world of words and their meanings for young children. Packed with photographs and lively illustrations, this book is designed to encourage children to practice using a dictionary, and to learn more about the language they use every day.

About this book

Each of the 1,000 headwords featured in **My First Dictionary** has been carefully selected from words commonly used by young children. Every headword is clearly defined in simple language and further defined with a full-color photograph or illustration. When teaching language and dictionary usage, it is essential to provide children with accurate visual clues to help them identify the word they want. With this in mind, every image in **My First Dictionary** has been carefully chosen to help young children understand each word.

Learning the alphabet

In the beginning, this dictionary will be a book to share with your child. Young children need to know the letters of the alphabet and understand alphabetical order as soon as they begin learning. This picture dictionary is an ideal tool for discovering how the alphabet works.

While you are looking at the pictures, point to the highlighted letter (picked out on white) in the alphabet strip at the top of each page. Then point to each word as you name the pictures. In this way children will learn that there are groups of words that begin with the same letter, and sometimes the same sound.

Learning to read and spell

As children develop into more competent readers, they will enjoy using **My First Dictionary** independently. Children will be able to find out for themselves what a particular word means, or how to spell it. However, this goal is best achieved with the support of parents and teachers.

Learning to use a dictionary

There is an exciting selection of word games at the back of this book. These games have been specially devised to help children understand the purpose of a dictionary and to become confident users. By working through these language games together, you will encourage your child to learn dictionary skills through play.

To broaden children's vocabulary, there are more than 150 additional words that appear in **bold** type in some of the definitions, or that can be found in some of the picture labels. These words are listed in an index on page 96. This index provides young readers with the possibility of gaining cross-referencing skills, which will help them to work confidently with other dictionaries.

By looking at the pages of **My First Dictionary** with young children, you will provide them with a head start in reading and writing, and an enjoyable look at language.

Betty Root, Author

act

To **act** is to pretend to be someone else. An **actor** is a person who acts in a play in front of an audience. Some actors act in television shows and movies.

airplane

An **airplane** is a flying machine with wings. It flies people and packages quickly from one place to another.

above

When something is **above** something else, it is higher up. These birds are flying above the trees.

add

$$2+2=4$$

To **add** is to find the sum total of two or more numbers.

airport

An **airport** is a place where airplanes take off and land.

accident

An **accident** is something that happens by mistake.

address

William Gray
437 Elm Avenue
Maplewood NJ 07040
U.S.A.

An **address** is the number of the building, the name of the street, town, state, and zip code where a person lives or works.

alligator

An **alligator** is a reptile with thick, scaly skin and lots of sharp **teeth.**

acrobat

An **acrobat** is a performer who can do difficult balancing tricks. Some acrobats can balance on their heads or walk on their hands.

adult

An **adult** is a grown-up person. **Men** and **women** are adults. When you are older, you will become an adult.

alphabet

abcdefg

English alphabet

абвгдеж

Russian alphabet

An **alphabet** is a list of all the letters we use to write words. Different languages have different alphabets.

ambulance

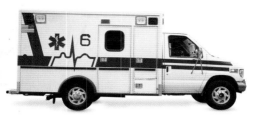

An **ambulance** is a special van or car that is used to carry sick or injured people to a hospital.

anchor

An **anchor** is a large, metal hook on a long chain. It digs into the bottom of the sea to stop a ship from moving.

angry

An **angry** person is someone who feels very upset about something.

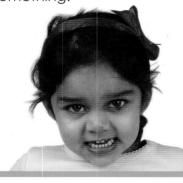

animal

An **animal** is any living thing that is not a plant. You are an animal, and so is a fish, spider, bird, snake, and dog.

spider

fish

bird

snake

dog

girl

ant

An **ant** is a tiny insect. Ants live in nests under the ground.

ape

An **ape** is an animal that is similar to a monkey, but without a tail.

apple

An **apple** is a fruit that grows on an apple tree.

aquarium

An **aquarium** is a tank of water in which fish, other water creatures, and plants are kept.

arm

Your **arm** is the part of your body between your shoulder and your hand.

armadillo

An **armadillo** is an animal covered with hard, bony scales. These scales protect the armadillo from attack.

armor

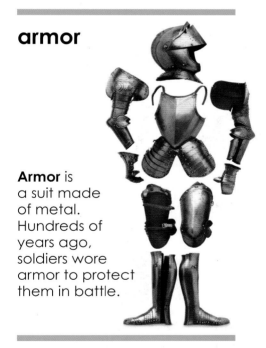

Armor is a suit made of metal. Hundreds of years ago, soldiers wore armor to protect them in battle.

army

An **army** is a large group of soldiers who are trained to fight on land in times of war.

arrow

An **arrow** is a sign that points the way.

artist

An **artist** is a person who creates art. Some artists draw or paint pictures. Other artists make pots out of clay, or statues out of stone.

astronaut

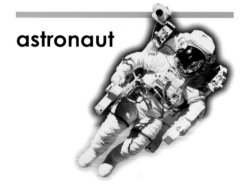

An **astronaut** is a person who travels to outer space in a spacecraft. Some astronauts have walked on the surface of the moon.

athlete

An **athlete** is a person who is good at sports, such as running, jumping, or swimming. Athletes take part in races or competitions.

audience

An **audience** is a group of people watching a performance together.

author

An **author** is a person who writes stories or other texts.

avalanche

An **avalanche** is a sudden fall of snow and rocks down the side of a mountain.

baby

A **baby** is a very young child.

back

The **back** of something is the part behind the front.

back

Your **back** is the part of your body that is behind your chest. Your back is between your neck and your bottom.

bake

To **bake** something is to cook it in an oven. A **baker** is a person who makes bread and desserts in a **bakery**.

ball

A **ball** is used to play many games and sports. Most balls are round.

balloon

A **balloon** is a thin rubber bag that is blown up with air or another kind of gas.

banana

A **banana** is a long, curved fruit with yellow skin. Bananas grow in bunches on banana plants.

band

A **band** is a group of people playing musical instruments together.

bandage

A **bandage** is a strip of material that is used to cover an injury.

bank

A **bank** is the high ground on both sides of a river or a stream.

bank

A **bank** is a safe place where you can keep money. You can take your money out again when you need it.

barbecue

A **barbecue** is a meal you cook outside on an open fire.

barn

A **barn** is a large farm building where a farmer keeps machinery or animals.

baseball

Baseball is a game played with a bat and ball by two teams of nine players.

basket

A **basket** is a kind of container for carrying things.

bat

A **bat** is a kind of stick that is used to hit a ball.

bat

A **bat** is a small, furry animal with wings. Bats hang upside down to sleep during the day. They hunt for food at night.

bathtub

A **bathtub** is a container that you fill with water and sit in to wash yourself. A bathtub is in the **bathroom.**

battery

A **battery** is a sealed case that makes electricity.

beach

A **beach** is a strip of land by the edge of a body of water. Beaches are covered with sand or pebbles.

beak

A **beak** is the hard, pointed part of a bird's mouth.

bear

A **bear** is a large, heavy animal with thick fur and strong claws.

beard

A **beard** is the hair that grows on a man's chin and cheeks.

bed

A **bed** is a piece of furniture that you sleep on. A **bedroom** is the room where you go to sleep.

bee

A **bee** is a flying insect. Some bees collect nectar, the sweet liquid in flowers, and turn it into honey.

beetle

A **beetle** is an insect. Beetles have hard, shiny wing cases to protect the soft parts of their bodies. Most beetles can fly.

behind

When something is **behind** something else, it is at the back of it. This girl is standing behind the door.

bell

A **bell** is a hollow piece of metal shaped like a cup. When you shake a bell, it rings.

below

When something is **below** something else, it is lower down. This bulb is growing below the surface of the **soil**.

surface of soil

bulb

belt

A **belt** is a strap that you wear around your **waist.**

bench

A **bench** is a **seat** for more than one person.

berry

A **berry** is a soft, juicy, fruit without a pit.

between

When you are **between** two things, you are in the middle of them. This boy is lying between the two dogs.

bicycle

A **bicycle** is a machine with two wheels that are moved around by **pedals.** To ride a **bike** you sit on the **seat**, pedal with your **feet**, and steer using the **handlebars.**

handlebars

seat

pedal

wheel

training wheels

big

When something is **big,** it is not small. The yellow ball is bigger than the blue ball.

binoculars

Binoculars are a special kind of glasses. They make things that are far away look bigger and closer.

bird

A **bird** is an animal with feathers, two wings, and a beak. Most birds can fly.

birthday

Your **birthday** is the day of the year when you were born. You may get birthday cards and eat birthday cake on this special day.

bite

To **bite** something is to take hold of it with your **teeth.**

black

Black is a very dark color. It is the opposite of white.

blanket

A **blanket** is a thick cover that keeps you warm in bed.

blind

A person who is **blind** cannot see. **Guide dogs** help blind people get around safely.

blood

Blood is the red liquid that is pumped around your body by your heart.

blossom

A **blossom** is a flower of a plant or a tree.

apple blossom

blouse

A **blouse** is clothing worn by a girl or a woman on the top part of her body.

blow

To **blow** is to push air quickly out of your mouth. This boy is blowing bubbles.

blue

Blue is the color of the sky on a sunny day.

boat

A **boat** is a small ship. Some boats carry people and cargo (things to be sold) across the water.

body

head
shoulder
hand
arm
chest
leg
foot

Your **body** is every part of you.

bone

A **bone** is one of the pieces of a skeleton. You have 206 different bones in your body.

book

A **book** is a collection of pages held together between two covers. There are words and pictures printed on the pages of a book.

b c d e f g h i j k l m n o p q r t u v w x y z

boomerang

A **boomerang** is a flat, curved piece of wood. When you throw a boomerang, it turns around in the air and comes back to you.

bottle

A **bottle** is a glass or plastic container for drinks and other liquids.

bottom

The **bottom** of something is the lowest part of it.

bowl

A **bowl** is a deep, round dish to put food in.

box

A **box** is a container with straight sides, a bottom, and sometimes a top.

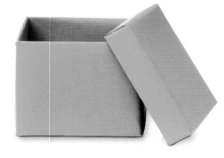

boy

A **boy** is a **male** child.

brain

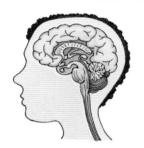

Your **brain** is inside your head. You think with your brain and it controls your body.

branch

A **branch** is the part of a tree that grows from the tree's **trunk.**

branch

trunk

bread

Bread is a food that is made from a mixture of water, flour or meal, and sometimes yeast.

break

When something **breaks**, it often cracks into pieces.

breakfast

Breakfast is the first meal that you eat in the day.

brick

A **brick** is a block of baked, hard clay used for building.

bride

A **bride** is a woman who is getting married. The man she is marrying is the **bridegroom.** After the wedding, they are **wife** and **husband.**

bridge

A **bridge** is a road that is built over rivers or railroads so that people can get across.

bulldozer

A **bulldozer** is a powerful machine that is used to move heavy rocks and **soil**.

brown

Brown is a color. Wood and **soil** are often brown.

building

A **building** is a place with walls and a roof, where people live or work. **Builders** use bricks, concrete, stones, or wood to **build** buildings.

burglar

A **burglar** is a person who breaks into a building to steal something.

brush

A **brush** is a tool that has a lot of bristles. A **hairbrush** is used to brush your hair. Other kinds of brushes are used to sweep or paint.

burn

To **burn** something is to set it on fire.

bucket

A **bucket** is a container with a handle that is used to hold water or other things.

bulb

A **bulb** is a part of some plants. It grows underground.

bulb

A light **bulb** uses electricity to create light.

bud

A **bud** is a young leaf or flower before it opens.

bus

A **bus** is a large vehicle that carries a lot of people. The bus **driver** stops at a **bus stop** to let the passengers on and off.

butcher

A **butcher** is a person who cuts up meat and sells it.

butter

A **Butter** is a yellow, fatty food that is made from cream.

butterfly

A **butterfly** is a flying insect with four colorful wings.

button

A **button** is a small object used for fastening clothes.

buy

To **buy** is to give money for something so that it belongs to you. The blond boy is buying groceries.

Cc

cabbage

A **cabbage** is a vegetable with tightly packed leaves.

cabin

A **cabin** is a wooden house, often made from logs.

cactus

A **cactus** is a prickly plant that grows in the desert. Most cacti store water in their thick stems.

calculator

A **calculator** is a machine that you use to work with numbers.

calendar

A **calendar** is a chart that shows what day it is. Calendars also show the month and the year.

camel

A **camel** is a large animal with one or two humps on its back. Camels live in hot, dry deserts.

camera

A **camera** is what you use to take photographs.

camp

To **camp** is to live outside. A **campsite** is a place where you set up your outdoor equipment.

can

A **can** is a sealed, metal container for storing food.

candle

A **candle** is a stick of wax with a string through the middle. When you burn a candle, it gives off a bright light.

canoe

A **canoe** is a long, narrow boat that is moved through water with a paddle.

cap

A **cap** is a soft hat. This is a baseball cap.

car

A **car** is a vehicle with four wheels and an engine. People travel in cars from one place to another. A **parking lot** is a place where a lot of cars can park.

carnation

A **carnation** is a flower with lots of petals. It can be various colors.

carpenter

A **carpenter** is a person who builds things out of wood. Some carpenters build houses. Other carpenters make furniture.

carrot

A **carrot** is a long vegetable that grows underground.

carry

To **carry** something is to take it from one place to another.

castle

A **castle** is a large building with thick, stone walls and tall towers. Castles were built hundreds of years ago to keep people safe from their enemies. Kings and queens lived in castles.

cat

A **cat** is a furry animal that is often kept as a pet.

catch

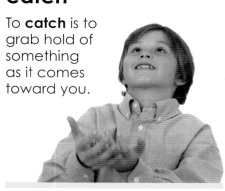

To **catch** is to grab hold of something as it comes toward you.

caterpillar

A **caterpillar** is a hairy insect that turns into a butterfly or a moth.

cauliflower

A **cauliflower** is a vegetable with green leaves and a white middle.

cave

A **cave** is a large hole in the side of a rock or under the ground.

centipede

A **centipede** is a tiny animal with many pairs of legs.

cereal

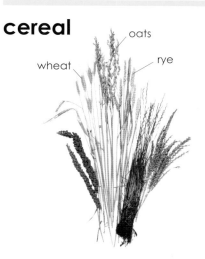

oats

wheat

rye

Cereal is a kind of grass that is grown for its seeds. The seeds are used to make food, such as flour or breakfast cereal.

chair

A **chair** is a piece of furniture for one person to sit on.

champion

A **champion** is a person who wins a game or contest in some sport.

chase

To **chase** is to run after someone or something. These children are chasing the ball.

cheap

$1.00

$20.00

When something is **cheap**, you can buy it with a small amount of money.

chameleon

A **chameleon** is a type of lizard. It can change the color of its skin to match the leaves and branches it is sitting on.

check out

When you **check out**, you take your items to a counter to pay for them.

cheer

To **cheer** is to shout and wave your hands with excitement.

cheese

Cheese is a food made from milk.

cheetah

A **cheetah** is a large, wild cat with a spotted coat. A cheetah can run faster than any other animal in the world.

chess

Chess is a game played on a chessboard.

chest

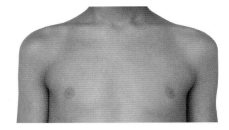

Your **chest** is the front part of your body, between your neck and your stomach.

chicken

rooster

hen

chicks

A **chicken** is a type of farm bird. A female chicken is called a **hen**, a male chicken is called a **rooster**, and a baby chicken is called a **chick**.

child

A **child** is a young boy or girl. **Children** grow up to become adults.

chimney

A **chimney** is a long pipe on top of a building. It takes away the smoke from a fire. This kind of chimney is called a **smokestack**.

chimpanzee

A **chimpanzee** is a kind of ape. Chimpanzees live in groups and play games together like humans do.

chin

Your **chin** is the part of your face below your mouth.

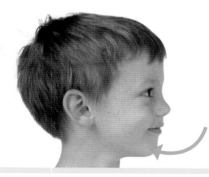

chocolate

Chocolate is a sweet food made from cocoa plant seeds.

choir

A **choir** is a large group of people who sing together.

choose

To **choose** something is to pick it instead of any other.

chopstick

Chopsticks are two thin sticks that are used to pick up and eat food.

church

A **church** is a building where Christian people meet to pray and sing hymns.

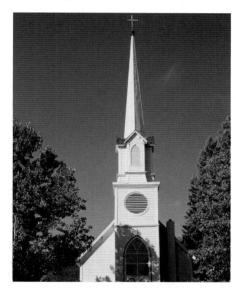

circle

A **circle** is a type of shape. Circles are round.

city

A **city** is a large town with lots of buildings where people live and work.

clap

To **clap** is to bring your hands together and make a loud noise.

claw

A **claw** is the sharp, hooked nail on the foot of a bird or an animal.

clean

When something is **clean**, it is not dirty. One boot is clean, but the other is muddy.

cliff

A **cliff** is a high, steep rock face.

climb

To **climb** is to go to the top of something using your hands and feet.

clock

A **clock** is a machine that shows the time of day.

clothes

pants   dress   shirt

skirt

Clothes are the things that people wear. Clothes are usually made from **cloth**.

cloud

A **cloud** is made out of drops of water floating in the sky.

clown

A **clown** is a funny person who makes people laugh. Clowns wear colorful clothes and paint their faces.

coat

A **coat** is an item of clothing that you wear outside to keep yourself warm.

cobweb

A **cobweb** is a net made by a spider to catch flies.

cockpit

A **cockpit** is the part of an airplane where the pilot sits. All the controls for flying the airplane are in the cockpit.

coconut

A **coconut** is a hard-shelled fruit with white flesh and coconut milk inside. Coconuts grow on coconut palm trees.

coffee

Coffee is a drink made from the brown seeds of the coffee bush. Many people drink hot coffee in the morning or at the end of a meal.

coffee seeds (known as coffee beans)

cold

When something is **cold**, it is not hot. When the weather is cold you may feel chilly and wear a coat.

color

Red, blue, and yellow are **colors**, and there are many other colors, bright, dark, and light.

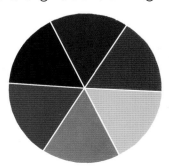

compact disc

A **compact disc**, or **CD**, is a circle of aluminum-coated plastic that stores sounds and pictures. A **compact disc player** is a machine for playing some CDs.

computer

screen

mouse

keyboard

A **computer** is a machine that people use to write, work with numbers, and store information. You use a **keyboard** to bring up the information on the **screen.**

conductor

A **conductor** is a person who keeps an orchestra playing together.

cone

A **cone** is a solid shape that is round at one end and pointed at the other.

continent

A **continent** is a large piece of land. We divide the world into seven continents:
1 Africa,
2 Antarctica,
3 Asia,
4 Australia,
5 Europe,
6 North America,
7 South America.

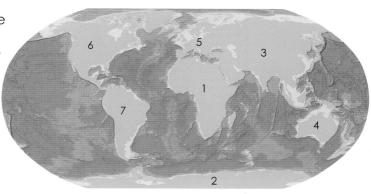

cook

To **cook** is to heat food and get it ready to eat.

corner

A **corner** is the point where two lines meet. This shape has three corners.

cotton

Cotton is the white fiber that grows on a cotton plant. Cotton is woven into **cloth.**

count

To **count** is to say numbers one after the other.

1   2   3

country

A **country** is a large area of land that is surrounded by borders and has its own special laws.

France

cousin

uncle

aunt

cousins

A **cousin** is a child of your aunt or uncle. An **aunt** is a sister of your mother or father. An **uncle** is a brother of your mother or father.

cow

cow

calf

A **cow** is a large farm animal that gives us milk to drink. Cows are female **cattle**. Male cattle are called **bulls** and young cattle are called **calves**.

crab

A **crab** is a sea animal with large claws on its front legs. Crabs have a hard shell to protect their soft bodies.

crane

A **crane** is a tall machine with a long arm that is used to lift heavy things.

crawl

To **crawl** is to move around on hands and knees.

crayon

A **crayon** is a stick of colored wax that you use for drawing.

cricket

Cricket is a team sport that is played with a cricket bat and ball.

cricket

A **cricket** is a small insect that chirps by rubbing its wings together.

crocodile

A **crocodile** is an animal with large jaws and a powerful tail that helps it swim.

crow

A **crow** is a type of bird. It has black feathers and a strong, black bill.

crowd

A **crowd** is a large number of people together in one place.

crown

A **crown** is a round headdress, often made of gold and jewels, worn by kings and queens.

crutch

A **crutch** is a long metal or wooden stick that helps you walk.

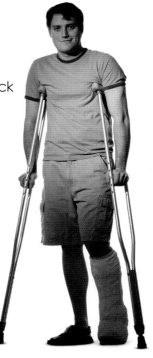

cry

When you **cry**, tears run down your face. Crying shows that you are sad or hurt.

cube

A **cube** is a solid shape with six square sides.

cucumber

A **cucumber** is a long, thin vegetable with bumpy, green skin.

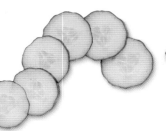

cup

A **cup** is a container that you drink from.

cupboard

A **cupboard** is a piece of furniture with doors on the front. People store things in a cupboard.

curtain

A **curtain** is a piece of material that hangs over or around a window. The curtain can be pulled across to cover the window.

cushion

A **cushion** is a bag full of soft material or feathers. We sit on cushions.

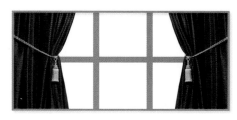

cut

To **cut** something is to slice it into pieces.

D d

daffodil

A **daffodil** is a yellow flower that grows from a bulb.

daisy

A **daisy** is a flower with white petals and a yellow center.

dam

A **dam** is a strong wall built across a river. A dam holds back water to make a lake.

dance

To **dance** is to move your body in time to music.

deer

A **deer** is a large, shy animal that can run very fast. A female deer is called a **doe,** and a young deer is called a **fawn.** Male deer are called **stags** and have **antlers.**

stags

antlers

dentist

A **dentist** is a person who takes care of your teeth.

dessert

A **dessert** is any kind of sweet food that you eat at the end of a meal.

dandelion

A **dandelion** is a yellow wild flower.

day

A **day** is 24 **hours** long. **Morning, afternoon, evening,** and night are all parts of one day.

morning

afternoon

evening

night

desert

A **desert** is a hot, dry, and sandy area of land.

detective

A **detective** is someone who hunts for clues and solves crimes and mysteries.

deaf

To be **deaf** is to have difficulty hearing. Some deaf people use sign language to talk to each other.

desk

A **desk** is a type of table that you sit at to read and write.

diagram

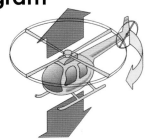

A **diagram** is a detailed drawing that explains how something works.

diamond

A **diamond** is a valuable stone that sparkles. It is clear like glass.

diary

A **diary** is a small notebook in which you write what has happened during your day.

dictionary

A **dictionary** is a book with a list of words and their meanings arranged in alphabetical order. This book is a dictionary.

different

When two things are **different**, they are not the same.

dinner

Dinner is the main meal of the day.

dinosaur

A **dinosaur** is a huge animal that lived millions of years ago. There are no more living dinosaurs.

dirty

When something is **dirty**, it is not clean. The dirty shoe is the one that is covered in mud.

disguise

A **disguise** is something you wear to hide who you are. Disguises make you look like someone else.

dive

To **dive** is to jump headfirst into water. A **diver** is a person who can dive.

doctor

A **doctor** is a person who helps sick or injured people get well.

dog

A **dog** is a furry animal with a tail that wags. Dogs are often kept as pets.

doll

A **doll** is a kind of toy. Dolls look like babies or miniature people.

dolphin

A **dolphin** is an animal that lives in the sea. Dolphins are friendly and intelligent animals.

donkey

A **donkey** is an animal that looks like a small horse. Donkeys have long ears and bray (cry out) loudly.

door

A **door** covers an entrance and can be opened and closed.

double

When something is **double**, it is twice as big or twice as many.

down

To move **down** is to go to a lower place. This train is traveling across the bridge and down the slope.

dragon

A **dragon** is an imaginary animal. Dragons have wings, and they breathe fire.

dragonfly

A **dragonfly** is a flying insect with a long, thin body and four wings.

draw

To **draw** is to make lines that form a picture.

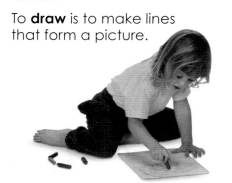

drawer

A **drawer** is a box that slides in and out of a **chest of drawers** or dresser.

dress

A **dress** is a piece of clothing worn by girls and **women.** The top and the skirt are joined together to make one piece.

dress

To **dress** yourself is to put on your clothes.

drill

A **drill** is a tool for making holes in wood, stone, or metal.

drink

To **drink** is to swallow a liquid, such as juice or water.

drive

To **drive** a vehicle is to operate and steer it. A **driver** is a person who can drive a vehicle.

drop

To **drop** something is to let it fall to the ground.

drum

A **drum** is a musical instrument that you play by hitting it with **drumsticks**.

dry

When you **dry** something, you stop it from being wet. This boy is drying a wet plate.

duck

drake

duck

duckling

A **duck** is a water bird. Ducks have webbed **feet** and a flat bill. A male duck is called a **drake** and a baby duck is called a **duckling.**

dump truck

A **dump truck** is a truck that is used to carry heavy loads of sand, **soil,** or stones. Its back lifts up so the load can be dumped out easily.

E e

eagle

An **eagle** is a large, powerful bird of prey.

ear

Your **ear** is a part of your head. You have two ears for hearing.

Earth

Earth is the planet where we live. The Earth is our world.

easel

An **easel** is a stand for holding a picture.

eat

To **eat** is to put food into your mouth, chew it, and swallow it.

egg

An **egg** is an unborn baby animal. Birds, insects, fish, and reptiles lay eggs. When an egg hatches, a baby animal comes out.

eight

Eight is the number that comes after seven and before nine.

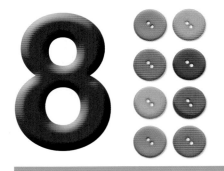

elbow

Your **elbow** is the middle joint in your arm.

elbow

electricity

Electricity is a powerful force. Electricity makes machines work and gives us light and heat.

elephant

An **elephant** is a huge, gray animal with a long trunk, large floppy ears, and two tusks.

empty

Something that is **empty** has nothing in it.

emu

An **emu** is a large bird with long legs. Emus cannot fly, but they can run very fast.

engine

An **engine** is a machine that makes things move or run. All cars have engines.

engineer

An **engineer** is someone who builds and fixes engines and machinery. Some engineers build bridges and buildings.

enter

To **enter** a building is to go into it through an **entrance**.

envelope

An **envelope** is a paper covering for a **letter**.

equal

When things are **equal,** they are the same size, number, or weight as each other. These scales show that the red apples and green apples are equal in weight.

equator

The **equator** is an imaginary line around the Earth, halfway between the **North Pole** and the **South Pole.**

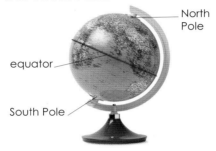

North Pole

equator

South Pole

escalator

An **escalator** is a moving staircase.

exercise

To **exercise** is to make your body stronger and fitter. This boy is exercising.

exit

The **exit** is the way out of a building.

expensive

When something is **expensive,** it costs a lot of money to buy.

$30

$2

explode

When something **explodes,** it blows up and makes a loud noise.

eye

Your **eyes** are a part of your face. You have two eyes for seeing.

F f

face

Your **face** is the front part of your head. Your eyes, nose, and mouth are parts of your face.

eyebrow — forehead
eye —
mouth — nose

factory

A **factory** is a building where people work together and use machines to make something.

fair

A **fair** is a place where people go to have fun. You can ride on a merry-go-round or a ferris wheel, and play games at the arcades.

fall

To **fall** is to drop to the ground.

family

A **family** is a group of people who are related to each other. A **mother, father, brother,** and **sister** are just one kind of family.

fan

A **fan** is a folded piece of paper that you wave to make a breeze.

farm

A **farm** is a piece of land for growing crops and keeping animals. A **farmer** is a person who works on a farm.

fast

When something moves **fast** it moves very quickly. This top is spinning fast.

fat

When something is **fat** it is not thin. One of these hamsters looks fat because its cheeks are packed with nuts.

feather

A **feather** is a covering that grows from a bird's skin.

fight

To **fight** is to battle against someone or something.

film

Film is a thin strip of material that can store images and sounds. It was often used to make movies and photographs, but today using **digital** images is more common.

finger

Your **finger** is a part of your hand. You have ten fingers.

fingerprint

A **fingerprint** is the mark made when you press your finger on something.

finish

To **finish** is to reach the end of something.

fire

A **fire** is heat, flames, and light made by something burning.

fire engine

A **fire engine** is a large truck that carries **firefighters**, hoses, and a water pump to a fire.

first aid

First aid is the help given to an injured person before a doctor arrives.

fish

A **fish** is a kind of animal that lives in water.

fish

To **fish** is to try to catch a fish.

five

Five is the number that comes after four and before six.

flag

A **flag** is a symbol of a country, club, or group of people. It is made from a large piece of **cloth** with a pattern on it.

flipper

A **flipper** is a kind of arm on an animal such as a sea lion or a penguin. Flippers are used for swimming or moving around on land.

flipper

float

When something **floats,** it stays on top of water or another liquid.

flood

A **flood** is a great flow of water that goes over dry land.

flour

Flour is a powder made from grain. It is used to make bread and cake.

flower

A **flower** is the colorful part of a plant or a tree. There are many different kinds of flowers.

flute

A **flute** is a long, thin musical instrument. You play a flute by blowing across a hole at one end and pressing the keys with your fingers.

fly

To **fly** is to move through the air like a bird, a kite, or an airplane.

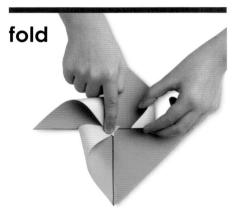

fly

A **fly** is a small, flying insect with two wings and six legs.

fog

Fog is a thick, gray cloud that hangs close to the ground.

fold

To **fold** something is to bend one part over the other part.

food

Food is what we eat. Food gives us energy and helps our bodies grow bigger and stronger.

foot

Your **foot** is the part of your body at the end of your leg. You have two **feet.**

football

A **football** is either an oval or a round ball. In many countries, people call soccer **football**.

footprint

A **footprint** is the mark made by a shoe or foot on the ground.

forest

A **forest** is a large area of land where lots of trees grow.

fork

A **fork** is a tool that is used to pick up food.

fossil

A **fossil** is the remains of an animal or plant that lived millions of years ago. Fossils are found in rocks.

fountain

A **fountain** is a jet of water that shoots up into the air.

four

Four is the number that comes after three and before five.

fox

A **fox** is a wild animal that looks like a dog with a long, bushy tail.

friend

A **friend** is someone who you like a lot.

frog

A **frog** is an animal that lives in and around water. Frogs have strong back legs for jumping.

fruit

Fruit is the juicy, seeded part of a plant. We eat fruit.

frying pan

A **frying pan** is a wide, flat, metal cooking dish with a handle.

full

When something is **full** it can hold no more.

fur

Fur is the thick, soft hair that grows on some animals and keeps them warm.

furniture

cupboard   table

sofa

chair   bed

Pieces of **furniture** are large moveable objects in a house or office. Chairs and tables are pieces of furniture.

G g

game

People play many different types of games. Each **game** has its own rules.

garage

A **garage** is a covered place where cars are parked.

garden

A **garden** is a place where lots of colorful flowers and vegetables are grown.

gate

A **gate** is a door in a fence or a wall.

ghost

A **ghost** is a dead person who some people think they can see, but many people think ghosts are make-believe.

giant

A **giant** is a huge, imaginary person.

giraffe

A **giraffe** is an animal with a very long neck and long, thin legs. Giraffes are the tallest animals in the world.

girl

A **girl** is a **female** child.

give

To **give** is to hand something to someone.

glass

Glass is a hard material that you can see through. It breaks easily.

glasses

Glasses are worn over your eyes if you need help to see better.

globe

A **globe** is a round ball with a map of the world printed on it.

glove

A **glove** is a warm covering for your hand.

glue

Glue is a liquid or paste that you use to stick things together.

goal

A **goal** is two posts with a net or an empty space between them. In some games, you kick a ball between the posts to score points.

goat

A **goat** is an animal with a beard under its chin and short horns. A female goat is called a **nanny**, a male goat is called a **billy**, and a young goat is called a **kid**.

nanny

kid

goggles

Goggles are special glasses that protect your eyes in the water.

gold

Gold is a precious yellow metal that can be made into **jewelry**. Gold is found in rocks.

goldfish

A **goldfish** is a small orange fish that is often kept as a pet.

golf

Golf is an outdoor game that is played with golf clubs and a golf ball. You use a club to hit a ball into a hole in the ground.

goose

A **goose** is a water bird with a short bill and a long neck. Male **geese** are called **ganders** and young geese are called **goslings**.

gander

gosling

gorilla

A **gorilla** is a big, strong ape.

grandparent

A **grandparent** is the parent of your mother or your father. Here are a **grandmother**, **grandfather**, and their **grandchildren**.

grape

A **grape** is a small, round fruit that grows in a bunch on a grapevine.

grapefruit

A **grapefruit** is a large, round, yellow or pink fruit.

grass

Grass is a green plant that covers the ground.

grasshopper

A **grasshopper** is a jumping insect with long, strong legs.

green

Green is a color. Many plants are green.

grow

To **grow** is to get bigger.

guitar

A **guitar** is a musical instrument with a long neck and strings. You play a guitar by strumming or plucking the strings.

gymnast

A **gymnast** is a person who does special exercises in a **gymnasium.**

H h

hair

Hair is the soft covering that grows on your head and body.

half

A **half** is one of two equal parts. Two **halves** make a whole.

hammer

A **hammer** is a tool that you use for knocking in nails.

hand

A **hand** is the part of the body below the wrist at the end of the arm. You hold things in your hand.

handle

A **handle** is the part of something that you hold.

hang

To **hang** something is to attach the top of it to a hook.

hangar

A **hangar** is a large building where airplanes are kept.

happy

A **happy** person is someone who is in a good mood.

harbor

A **harbor** is a sheltered place, on a coast, where ships and boats are kept safely.

hat

A **hat** is a covering for the head.

hawk

A **hawk** is a bird of prey. Hawks eat small animals such as rabbits and fish.

head

Your **head** is the part of your body that is above your neck.

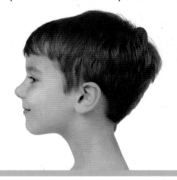

headlight

A **headlight** is a light on the front of a car or truck.

hearing aid

A **hearing aid** is a machine that you wear in your ear if you have difficulty hearing.

heart

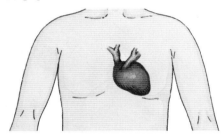

Your **heart** is an organ inside your chest. It pumps blood around your body.

heavy

If something is **heavy**, it weighs a lot and is difficult to move.

heel

Your **heel** is at the back of your foot.

helicopter

A **helicopter** is a flying machine that has a large propeller on top to make it hover in the air.

helmet

A **helmet** is a hard hat that protects your head.

help

To **help** someone is to make their job easier.

hibernate

When an animal **hibernates**, it sleeps through the cold, winter months. Ground squirrels and woodchucks hibernate.

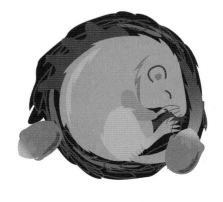

hide

To **hide** is to put something in a place where no one can see it. This boy is hiding himself behind the sofa.

high

When something is **high**, it is not low. These hot air balloons are high in the sky.

hill

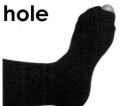

A **hill** is a big hump in the land. Hills are smaller than mountains.

hip

Your **hip** is the bony part of your body that sticks out just below your **waist.** Your legs join your body at your hips.

hippopotamus

A **hippopotamus** is a large animal with very thick skin and short legs. It likes to wallow in muddy water.

hold

To **hold** something is to have it in your hands or arms.

hole

A **hole** is an opening in something.

honey

Honey is a sweet, sticky syrup that is made by bees.

hoof

A **hoof** is the hard covering on the **feet** of some animals.

hop

To **hop** is to jump up and down on one leg.

horn

A **horn** is something that makes a loud noise to warn people of danger.

horse

A **horse** is a large animal with a mane, tail, and hooves. A female horse is called a **mare**, a male horse is called a **stallion**, and a baby horse is called a **foal.**

hospital

A **hospital** is a place where doctors and nurses take care of sick or injured people.

hot

When something is **hot**, it is not cold. This cup of coffee is very hot.

37

hotel

A **hotel** is a place where people pay to stay in bedrooms. Many hotels also have restaurants.

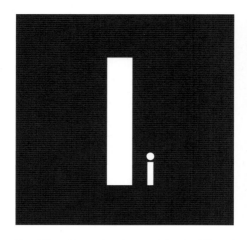

house

A **house** is a building where people live.

hutch

A **hutch** is a pet rabbit's house.

ice

Ice is frozen water.

hyena

A **hyena** is a wild animal that looks like a wolf. A hyena's call sounds like a loud, human laugh.

hug

To **hug** something is to put your arms around it and hold it tightly.

iceberg

An **iceberg** is a very large piece of ice that floats in the ocean.

hundred

A **hundred** is the number that comes after 99 and before 101.

ice cream

Ice cream is a frozen dessert made from cream and eggs.

icicle

An **icicle** is a hanging piece of ice made by water freezing as it drips.

igloo

An **igloo** is a house made from blocks of snow and ice.

iguana

An **iguana** is a large lizard with a long tail and a ridge of spines along its back. Some iguanas live in trees.

injection

An **injection**, or a shot, is a way that a doctor or nurse can give you a vaccine or medicine. A needle is pricked into your skin, and the medicine is pushed through the needle into your body.

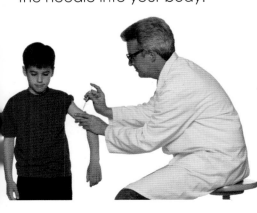

injure

To **injure** yourself is to hurt yourself. This girl hurt her leg.

insect

An **insect** is a tiny animal with six legs. Most insects have wings.

inside

When something is **inside**, it is within and not outside. These shoes are inside a shoebox.

instrument

An **instrument** is something that makes musical sounds.

saxophone

Internet

The **Internet** is a computer network that shares information and connects people all over the world.

invent

To **invent** is to make something that did not exist before. An **inventor** invents things.

invite

To **invite** someone is to ask them to a party or another event. An **invitation** is the card that you send.

Please come to my party!

iron

An **iron** is a hot tool that takes the creases out of clothes.

island

An **island** is a piece of land with water all around it.

ivy

Ivy is a plant that grows up walls and trees.

J j

jacket

A **jacket** is a short coat.

jaguar

A **jaguar** is a large, wild cat with a spotted coat.

jam

Jam is a sweet food that you spread on bread. It is made by boiling fruit with sugar.

jar

A **jar** is a glass container with a wide neck and a lid.

jaw

Your **jaw** is the bony part of your mouth that holds your **teeth**. You move your lower jaw when you chew.

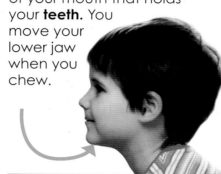

jeans

Jeans are **pants** made out of strong, cotton **cloth**.

jellyfish

A **jellyfish** is a sea animal that has a soft body and long tentacles.

jewel

emerald

A **jewel** is a precious stone, such as an **emerald** or a **ruby**. Jewels are used to make sparkling **jewelry**.

jigsaw puzzle

A **jigsaw puzzle** is a picture cut up into pieces that you have to fit together again.

judo

Judo is a fighting sport using holds and throws.

jug

A **jug**, or **pitcher**, is a container with a handle and a spout for pouring liquids.

juggle

To **juggle** is to keep several objects in the air by throwing and catching them quickly. A **juggler** is a person who can juggle.

juice

Juice is the liquid that comes out of fruit.

jump

To **jump** is to leap into the air so both **feet** leave the ground.

jungle

A **jungle** is a hot, steamy forest where it rains a lot. There are lots of tall trees in a jungle. Jungles can be called **rain forests.**

K k

kangaroo

A **kangaroo** is an animal with long, powerful back legs, which it uses for jumping. A female kangaroo carries her baby in her pouch.

karate

Karate is a fighting sport using foot kicks and hand chops.

kennel

A **kennel** is a house for a pet dog.

key

A **key** is a metal tool for locking or unlocking doors.

kick

To **kick** is to hit out with your foot.

king

A **king** is a man who rules a country. Kings live in palaces.

kiss

To **kiss** is to touch something with your lips.

kitchen

A **kitchen** is the room where food is cooked.

knit

To **knit** is to join loops of yarn to make clothes and other things. You knit with knitting needles.

kite

A **kite** is a toy that you fly in the wind.

kneel

To **kneel** is to go down on your knees.

knock

To **knock** is to tap something with your knuckles to make a noise.

kitten

A **kitten** is a young cat.

knife

A **knife** is a tool with a sharp blade used for cutting.

knot

A **knot** is a fastening made by tying things together. This is a knot in a piece of rope.

knight

Knights were brave soldiers who lived a long time ago. Knights rode horses and wore armor.

knee

Your **knee** is the joint in the middle of your leg. Your leg bends at your knee.

koala

A **koala** is a furry animal with big ears and a black nose. Koalas eat eucalyptus leaves and live in trees.

L l

laboratory

A **laboratory** is a place where people learn about science and do experiments.

ladder

A **ladder** is a tall climbing frame with lots of steps. You climb ladders to reach high places.

ladybug

A **ladybug** is a tiny insect that often has spotted wing cases.

lake

A **lake** is a large area of water surrounded by land.

lamb

A **lamb** is a young sheep.

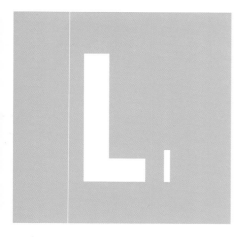

lamp

A **lamp** is a stand for a bulb that is covered by a lampshade. A lamp gives off light.

land

Land is the part of the Earth that is not water. We live on land.

large

When something is **large**, it is not little. This large doll contains all the little dolls.

laugh

To **laugh** is to make sounds that show you are happy.

lawn

A **lawn** is a piece of ground that is covered with grass. A lawn is cut with a **lawnmower.**

leaf

A **leaf** is a flat, green part of a plant that grows from its stem.

lean

To **lean** is to tilt your body to one side.

left

Left is the opposite of right. This girl is about to make a left turn on her bicycle.

leg

Your **leg** is the part of your body between your bottom and your foot. People walk on two legs.

lemon

A **lemon** is a yellow fruit with a very sour taste.

leopard

A **leopard** is a wild cat that has sharp **teeth** and claws. Leopards have a yellow coat with black spots.

letter

A **letter** is a part of the alphabet. You put letters together to make words.

lettuce

Lettuce is a leafy, green vegetable that you eat in a salad.

library

A **library** is a place where lots of books are kept on shelves. You can borrow books from most libraries.

lick

To **lick** something is to touch it with your tongue.

lifeboat

A **lifeboat** is a type of boat that is used to rescue people at sea.

lift

To **lift** something is to pick it up. This boy is lifting up the bucket.

light

If something is **light,** it is not heavy. Light things weigh very little and are easy to lift.

lighthouse

A **lighthouse** is a tall tower, on the coast, with a bright light on the top. Lighthouses warn ships of danger.

lightning

Lightning is a flash of light that appears in the sky during a **thunderstorm.**

lion

A **lion** is a fierce, big cat that roars. A male lion has a shaggy **mane** around its head. A female lion is called a **lioness.**

lioness

mane

lion

lip

Your **lips** are the soft, fleshy edges around your mouth.

liquid

A **liquid** is wet and can be poured. Orange juice is a liquid.

litter

Litter is the garbage that should be recycled or put in the garbage.

little

When something is **little,** it is not large. The purple flower is little.

lizard

A **lizard** is a reptile with a long, scaly body, a tail, and four short legs.

lobster

A **lobster** is a sea animal with a hard shell, ten legs, and large claws on its front legs.

lock

A **lock** is a fastening that you open with a key. This is a **padlock.**

log

A **log** is a thick piece of wood that has been cut from a tree.

45

long

When something is **long**, it measures a lot from end to end. One of these strings of beads is long and one is short.

low

When something is **low**, it is not high. This girl is low down in the grass.

look

To **look** is to use your eyes to see things.

luggage

Luggage is all the bags and suitcases that you take on vacation.

machine

A **machine** is an object with parts that move together to make something work. Clocks, cars, bicycles, and computers are all machines.

lose

When you **lose** something, you cannot find it. This girl has lost a shoe.

lunch

Lunch is the meal that you eat in the middle of the day.

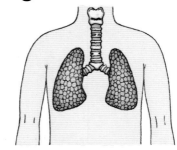

magazine

A **magazine** is a collection of pages of articles and pictures, usually about a certain subject, printed every week or month.

love

To **love** is to like someone or something very much.

lung

Your **lungs** are inside your chest. You have two lungs for breathing.

magic

Magic is a way of doing amazing tricks that seem to be impossible. A **magician** is a person who can do magic tricks.

magnet

A **magnet** is a piece of **iron** or **steel** that can pull other pieces of iron or steel toward it.

magnifying glass

A **magnifying glass** is a special piece of glass that makes things look bigger than they really are.

mammal

A **mammal** is a warm-blooded animal that feeds on its mother's milk.

man

A **man** is a grown-up boy.

map

A **map** is a drawing of part of the Earth's surface. This map of the world shows where the countries are.

market

A **market** is a place where people buy and sell things.

mask

A **mask** is a covering for your face. You wear a mask to disguise yourself.

match

A **match** is a short stick that makes a flame when you rub it on a rough surface.

mathematics

Mathematics is the study of numbers, shapes, and sizes.

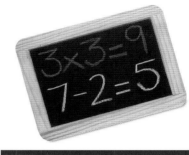

meal

A **meal** is the food that you eat at one time.

measure

To **measure** something is to find out what size it is.

meat

Meat is the part of an animal that is eaten as food.

mechanic

A **mechanic** is a person who makes and repairs cars or other machines.

microscope

A **microscope** is an instrument that makes tiny things look bigger.

medal

A **medal** is a piece of metal, often round, given to a person who wins a competition.

melt

When something **melts** it turns to liquid as it warms up.

metal

Metal is a hard material, such as **copper, iron,** or **steel.** Metals are found in rocks and used to make things.

rock containing copper

copper pipe

microwave oven

A **microwave oven** is a machine for cooking food very quickly.

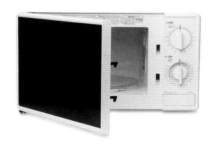

medicine

Medicine is a pill or a liquid that you swallow to make you better if you are sick.

midday

Midday is the middle of the day. You eat your lunch at midday.

12:00

meet

To **meet** someone is to come face to face with them.

microphone

A **microphone** is an instrument that makes your voice louder.

midnight

Midnight is the middle of the night. You are asleep at midnight.

milk

Milk is a white liquid that some animals make to feed their babies. Many people drink cow's milk.

mine

A **mine** is a deep hole under the ground where people dig for rocks, such as coal.

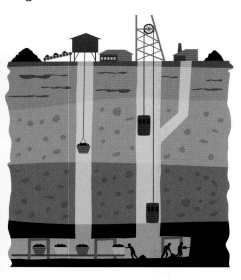
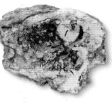

mineral

Minerals can be found in rocks, and are dug out of mines.

mirror

A **mirror** is a special piece of glass in which you can see your reflection.

mix

To **mix** things is to stir them together.

money

Money is the coins and paper bills that we use to buy things.

monkey

Monkeys are furry animals with long arms and long legs. Most monkeys also have long tails for swinging in trees.

monster

A **monster** is a make-believe creature that looks strange and frightening. You can read about monsters in fairy tales.

month

A **month** is a measure of time that is about 30 days long. There are 12 months in a year.

JANUARY
FEBRUARY
MARCH
APRIL
MAY
JUNE
JULY
AUGUST
SEPTEMBER
OCTOBER
NOVEMBER
DECEMBER

moon

The **moon** is the Earth's satellite. It shines in the sky at night.

moose

A **moose** is a large deer. Moose have long faces, and male moose have huge **antlers.**

mosque

A **mosque** is a building where Muslim people meet to pray.

mosquito

A **mosquito** is a flying insect that bites your skin to suck your blood.

moth

A **moth** is an insect that looks like a butterfly. It flies around at night.

motorcycle

A **motorcycle** is a machine that you ride. This motorcycle has a powerful engine.

mountain

A **mountain** is a very high, rocky hill.

mouse

A **mouse** is a small, furry animal with a long tail. **Mice** live in nests.

mouse

A **mouse** is a small device that you can use to move a pointer on a computer **screen.**

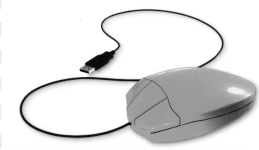

mouth

Your **mouth** is part of your face. You use your mouth for eating and speaking.

mud

Mud is wet, soft earth.

muscle

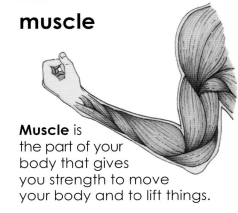

Muscle is the part of your body that gives you strength to move your body and to lift things.

museum

A **museum** is a building where you can see old things and works of art.

50

mushroom

A **mushroom** is a fungus that is shaped like a small umbrella. You can eat some mushrooms, but others are poisonous.

music

Music is the notes that you read, or the sound that you make, when you are singing or playing an instrument.

musician

A **musician** is a person who can make music by playing a musical instrument.

N n

nail

A **nail** is a small, metal spike with a sharp point at one end. You hammer nails into wood.

narrow

When something is **narrow**, it is not wide. Narrow spaces are difficult to squeeze through.

navy

A **navy** is a large group of warships carrying sailors who are trained to fight at sea in times of war.

neck

Your **neck** is the part of your body that is between your head and your shoulders.

needle

A **needle** is a thin, pointed piece of metal that you use for sewing.

nest

A **nest** is a home where an animal lives and cares for its babies.

net

Net is material made from loosely knotted string. You can catch fish in a **fishing net.**

new

When something is **new**, it is not old. New things have just been made or bought.

newspaper

A **newspaper** is a collection of printed sheets of paper. You read newspapers to find out about world events.

newt

A **newt** is an animal that lives in and around water.

night

Night is the time when it is dark outside. Night begins at sunset and ends at sunrise.

nine

Nine is the number that comes after eight and before ten.

noise

A **noise** is a loud sound. This girl is making noise on the tuba.

nose

Your **nose** is part of your face. You breathe and smell through your nose.

number

A **number** is a sign that tells you how many things there are.

0 1 2 3 4 5

nurse

A **nurse** is a person who is trained to take care of sick or injured people in a hospital.

nut

A **nut** is a small piece of metal that you screw onto a **bolt**. Nuts and bolts are used to hold things together.

nut

bolt

nut

A **nut** is a fruit or a seed with a hard shell.

nutcracker

A **nutcracker** is a tool used for breaking open nuts.

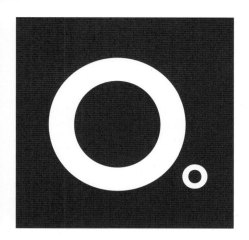

office

An **office** is a place where people go to work. There are desks, chairs, and computers in offices.

oar

An **oar** is a long pole with a flat blade at one end. You use oars to row a boat.

ocean

An **ocean** is a large body of salt water. The Pacific and the Atlantic are oceans.

octopus

An **octopus** is a sea animal with eight long arms and a soft, round body.

oil

Oil is a greasy liquid that makes machines run smoothly.

old

When something is **old** it is not new. Old things look used.

one

One is the number that comes before two. When you count, you start with the number one.

onion

An **onion** is a round vegetable that often makes your eyes water when it's cut open.

open

When something is **open** it is not shut or closed.

opera

An **opera** is a play in which the words are sung to music.

53

opposite

When things are the **opposite** of each other, they are completely different. Hot and cold are opposites, so are front and back.

optometrist

An **optometrist** is a person who tests your eyes to see if you need glasses.

orange

Orange is a color made by mixing red and yellow.

orange

An **orange** is a round, juicy fruit with a thick, orange-colored skin.

orangutan

An **orangutan** is a large ape with long fur and strong arms.

orchard

An **orchard** is an area of land where fruit trees are grown.

orchestra

An **orchestra** is a large group of musicians playing instruments together.

organ

An **organ** is a musical instrument with a keyboard, and long, metal pipes that make sounds when air is pushed through them.

ostrich

An **ostrich** is a large bird with a long neck, long legs, and big feathers. Ostriches cannot fly, but they can run very fast.

otter

An **otter** is a furry animal that lives in and around water.

outside

When something is **outside**, it is not inside. This puppy is outside its doghouse.

oval

An **oval** is a type of shape. Eggs are oval.

oven

An **oven** is a machine that cooks food.

owl

An **owl** is a bird with a large head and big, round eyes. Owls usually hunt for food at night.

oyster

An **oyster** is a sea animal with a soft body inside a hard shell. Some oysters make pearls inside their shells.

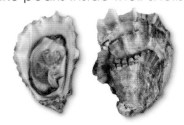

page

A **page** is one side of a sheet of paper in a book.

paint

To **paint** is to make a picture using a brush and paints.

paint

Paint is a colored liquid used to paint pictures.

pair

A **pair** is a set of two things that are used together, such as these socks.

palace

A **palace** is a very large, grand house where kings and queens sometimes live.

palm

Your **palm** is the inside part of your hand.

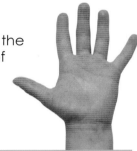

palm tree

A **palm tree** is a tree that grows in hot places. Palm trees have large leaves that grow at the top of a long trunk.

panda

A **panda** is a large, furry animal. Giant pandas look like bears with black-and-white fur.

panther

A **panther** is a large leopard with a black coat.

paper

Paper is a material used to write on.

parachute

A **parachute** is a large piece of material that is shaped like an umbrella. Parachutes help people float through air and land safely on the ground.

parcel

A **parcel**, or package, is a large item that is sent in the mail.

parent

A **parent** is a person who has a child. Your mother and father are your parents. You are their **son** or **daughter**.

park

A **park** is a piece of land where people can enjoy the open space and playgrounds.

parrot

A **parrot** is a bird with brightly colored feathers. Some parrots can be trained to repeat words.

party

A **party** is a group of people who come together to celebrate. You might have a party on your birthday.

passenger

A **passenger** is a person who travels in a bus or a car. Passengers don't drive.

path

A **path** is a trail for people to walk on.

patient

A **patient** is a person who is sick and is being cared for by a nurse or a doctor.

paw

A **paw** is an animal's foot.

pay

To **pay** for something is to give money for it.

pea

A **pea** is a small, round vegetable that grows in a pod.

peach

A **peach** is a sweet, juicy fruit with a soft skin, and a pit in the middle.

peacock

A **peacock** is a bird with colorful tail feathers that open out like a fan.

peanut

A **peanut** is a seed that grows in a pod in the soil.

pear

A **pear** is a fruit that narrows at the top and has tiny pits in the middle.

pearl

A **pearl** is a small, white gemstone that is found in some oyster shells. Pearls are used to make **jewelry**.

pebble

A **pebble** is a small, smooth stone found on the beach.

peel

Peel is the skin on some fruits and vegetables.

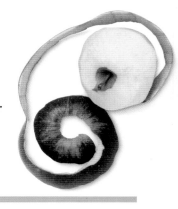

peel

To **peel** something is to take the skin off it. This boy is peeling a banana.

pelican

A **pelican** is a bird with a large pouch under its beak that it uses to catch fish to eat.

pen

A **pen** is a tool filled with ink used for writing.

pencil

A **pencil** is something you write or draw with. It is made of wood and graphite.

penguin

A **penguin** is a black-and-white seabird that cannot fly. Penguins use their wings (also called flippers) to swim in the water.

people

People are **men, women,** and **children.**

pepper

Pepper is a strong spice that is often ground up to flavor food.

perfume

Perfume is a sweet-smelling liquid made from flower petals and spices. You put perfume on your body.

pet

A **pet** is a tame animal that you take care of and keep at home.

petal

A **petal** is a part of a flower. It is often brightly colored.

photograph

A **photograph** is a picture taken with a camera.

photographer

A **photographer** is a person who takes photographs.

piano

A **piano** is a large musical instrument with black-and-white keys. You press the keys to make music.

picnic

A **picnic** is a meal that is eaten outside.

picture

When you create a **picture,** you draw or paint what something looks like.

pie

A **pie** is a pastry shell filled with fruit, meat, or vegetables, and baked in an oven.

pig

A **pig** is an animal with a short snout, a little tail, big ears, and bristly hairs on its skin. A male pig is called a **boar**, a female pig is called a **sow**, and a baby pig is called a **piglet**.

pigeon

A **pigeon** is a bird with a large, round body and a small head. Most pigeons live in cities.

pile

A **pile** is a lot of things stacked on top of one another.

pillow

A **pillow** is a bag of soft material for your head to rest on.

pilot

A **pilot** is a person who flies an airplane.

pin

A **pin** is a thin, pointed piece of metal used to hold **cloth** together.

pineapple

A **pineapple** is a large fruit with thick, bumpy skin and pointed leaves. The fruit inside is sweet and juicy.

pink

Pink is a color. It is made by mixing red and white.

pipe

A **pipe** is a hollow tube of metal or plastic. Liquid runs through pipes.

pirate

A **pirate** is a robber who steals from ships at sea.

planet

A **planet** is a huge, round mass, mostly made up of rock and metal, or gas, that moves around the sun or another star. Eight planets move around the sun.

Uranus

Jupiter

Neptune

Saturn

Mars

Earth

Mercury

Venus

plant

A **plant** is anything that grows in the **soil**. Flowers and trees are plants.

plastic

Plastic is a material made from chemicals. This blow-up toy is made out of plastic.

plate

A **plate** is a flat dish that you put food on.

play

To **play** is to do something for fun.

plum

A **plum** is a purple fruit with a pit in the middle.

plumber

A **plumber** is a person who works on and fixes pipes.

pocket

A **pocket** is a small bag that is sewn into your clothes.

point

A **point** is the sharp end of something. These objects all have sharp points.

polar bear

A **polar bear** is a huge bear covered in thick, white fur.

police officer

A **police officer** is a person who protects people and makes sure laws are obeyed.

polish

To **polish** is to rub something to make it shine.

pond

A **pond** is a small lake.

pony

A **pony** is a kind of small horse.

post office

A **post office** is a place where you can buy stamps and mail letters and packages. The letters and packages are sorted in a **sorting office**.

post office   sorting office

poppy

A **poppy** is a flower with big, red petals. Poppies grow from poppy seeds.

potato

A **potato** is a vegetable that grows in the ground.

price

The **price** of something is the amount of money you have to pay for it.

$10.50

porcupine

A **porcupine** is an animal with pointed hairs called quills.

pour

To **pour** a liquid is to tip it out of a container.

pricker

A **pricker** is a sharp point. This chestnut has prickers.

prince

A **prince** is the son of a king and queen. A **princess** is the daughter of a king and queen.

postcard

A **postcard** is used for sending a message by mail without an envelope. It usually has a picture on one side and space for a message, address, and stamp on the other side.

present

A **present** is something that you give to someone on a special occasion.

61

prize

A **prize** is a reward you may be given if you win a competition.

propeller

A **propeller** is a strong fan that spins around to drive airplanes and boats.

puddle

A **puddle** is a small pool of water.

pull

To **pull** is to take hold of something and move it toward you.

pump

A **pump** is a machine that forces liquid or gas into or out of something. This pump forces air into a bicycle tire.

puncture

A **puncture** is a small hole in something that lets air or water get out. This tire has a puncture.

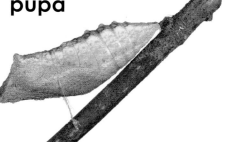

pupa

A **pupa** is a caterpillar while it is in a cocoon changing into a butterfly or a moth.

puppet

A **puppet** is a doll that is moved by strings or your fingers.

puppy

A **puppy** is a young dog.

purple

Purple is a color. It is made by mixing blue and red.

push

To **push** is to take hold of something and move it away from you.

puzzle

A **puzzle** is a game or a problem that you enjoy trying to figure out.

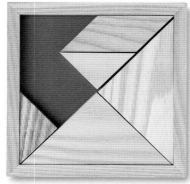

pyramid

A **pyramid** is a building with a square base and sloping, triangular sides. Ancient people built pyramids.

python

A **python** is a large snake that kills its prey by squeezing it to death.

Q q

quarry

A **quarry** is a place where stone is cut out of the ground. The stone is used to make buildings and other things.

quarter

A **quarter** is one of four equal parts. Four quarters make a whole.

queen

A **queen** is a woman who is a head of a country. Queens live in palaces.

quick

To be **quick** is to do something in a short time.

quiet

To be **quiet** is to make very little noise.

quilt

A **quilt** is a warm, soft covering for a bed.

quiz

A **quiz** is a game or a test where people try to answer questions.

R r

rabbit

A **rabbit** is a small, furry animal with long ears.

race

A **race** is a competition to find out who is the fastest.

race car

A **race car** is a type of car that goes very fast around a track.

radio

A **radio** is a machine that receives radio signals (called radio waves) from the air. It turns them into music or voices that you listen to on the radio.

raft

A **raft** is a flat boat that is made out of logs.

railroad

A **railroad** is a track for trains to run on. The track is made from long strips of metal called **rails**.

railroad station

A **railroad station** is a place where you go to buy a ticket and catch a train.

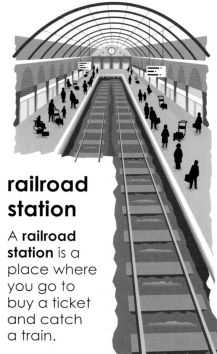

rain

Rain is drops of water that fall from clouds in the sky.

rainbow

A **rainbow** is an arc of different colors that appear in the sky when the sun shines through rain. The seven colors of the rainbow are: red, orange, yellow, green, blue, **indigo**, and **violet**.

reach

To **reach** for something is to stretch out your hand to take or touch it. This boy is reaching for a cookie.

read

To **read** is to understand the meaning of written or printed words.

recorder

A **recorder** is a wooden or plastic musical instrument. You play a recorder by blowing in it and covering the holes with your fingers.

rectangle

A **rectangle** is a shape with two long sides, two shorter sides, and four corners.

recycle

To **recycle** is to process things so that they can be reused. We recycle paper, glass, and metal to help the environment.

red

Red is a color. Tomatoes are often red.

refrigerator

A **refrigerator** is a storage container for food that has a machine inside that keeps it cold.

repair

To **repair** something is to fix it.

reptile

A **reptile** is a cold-blooded animal with a backbone. Most reptiles are covered with scales. Snakes and lizards are reptiles.

lizard

snake

rescue

To **rescue** someone or something is to save them from danger or harm.

restaurant

A **restaurant** is a place where you can buy and eat a meal.

rhinoceros

A **rhinoceros** is a large, heavy animal with a thick skin. It has one or two horns on the top of its nose.

ribbon

A **ribbon** is a thin strip of material that you use for decoration.

65

rice

Rice is the small, white seeds of a plant that grows in wet ground in hot countries. Rice makes a tasty meal.

ride

To **ride** is to sit in or on something while it moves. This girl is riding a horse.

right

Right is the opposite of left. This girl is making a right turn on her bicycle.

ring

A **ring** is a circle of metal that you wear on your finger.

ring

A **ring** is a sound we hear. Bells, telephones, and ears can all ring.

river

A **river** is a large stream of water that flows into another river, lake, or ocean.

road

A **road** is a hard, smooth track for cars, trucks, and other traffic to drive on. A **highway** is a type of road.

robot

A **robot** is a machine that can move and sometimes do jobs that people can do.

rock

A **rock** is a large stone found in the ground or in mountains.

rocket

A **rocket** flies by shooting fire or hot gases out one end. Rockets put spacecraft into space.

roll

To **roll** is to turn over and over as you move along.

roof

A **roof** is the part that covers the top of a building.

room

A **room** is part of a whole building. A room has a **ceiling**, a **floor**, four **walls**, and a door.

root

A **root** is the part of a plant that grows underground. Roots take up water from the **soil** to feed the plant.

root

rope

Rope is strong, thick string. Ropes are used to pull or lift heavy things.

rose

A **rose** is a sweet-smelling flower with lots of petals and thorns on its stem.

round

When something is **round**, it is shaped like a circle or a ball.

rug

A **rug** is a piece of material that covers part of a floor.

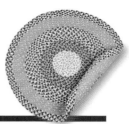

ruler

A **ruler** is a measuring tool that helps you find out how long something is.

run

To **run** is to move very quickly.

runway

A **runway** is a strip of flat, smooth ground where aircraft can take off and land.

row

A **row** is a straight line of things.

S s

sad

A **sad** person is someone who feels unhappy.

saddle

A **saddle** is the **seat** you sit on when you ride on a horse.

sail

A **sail** is a large piece of material attached to a boat. Wind blows into the sail to push the boat through the water.

sail

To **sail** is to travel on a boat. A **sailor** is a person who works on a boat. A **sailboat** is a boat that is moved by wind in its sails.

salad

A **salad** is usually cold, and is a mixture of foods, such as lettuce, tomatoes, and cucumber.

salt

Salt is a white powder made from minerals found in seawater. Salt is used to flavor food.

same

When two things are the **same**, they are like each other in every way.

sand

Sand is grains of rock that cover a beach or desert.

sandcastles

sandwich

A **sandwich** is two pieces of bread with food in between them.

satellite

A **satellite** is any object that moves around a planet in space. Mechanical satellites move around the Earth, collecting and sending information.

satellite dish

A **satellite dish** sends information to and receives information from a mechanical satellite.

saucepan

A **saucepan** is a metal container used for cooking.

saw

A **saw** is a tool that has a blade with sharp, metal **teeth.** You use a saw to cut wood.

scale

A **scale** is a hard, thin piece of skin on a fish or a reptile. This fish is covered with hundreds of scales.

scale

A **scale** is a machine that tells you how much things weigh.

scarf

A **scarf** is a long piece of material worn around your neck.

school

A **school** is a place where you go to learn. At school, your teacher teaches you important things, such as how to read, write, and count.

scientist

A **scientist** is a person who studies a science, such as chemistry.

scissors

Scissors are a tool with two sharp blades. You use scissors to cut things.

scorpion

A **scorpion** is an animal with two large claws and a poisonous stinger in its tail.

scratch

To **scratch** yourself is to rub your skin with your fingernails to stop your skin from itching.

screw

A **screw** holds things together. All screws have grooves in them.

scrub

To **scrub** something is to rub it with a wet brush to clean it. The potato is being scrubbed.

sea

The **sea** is the part of the Earth that is salt water. Another word for sea is ocean.

seagull

A **seagull** is a bird with gray-and-white feathers. You often see seagulls near the coast.

sea horse

A **sea horse** is a sea animal. It has a head that looks like a horse's head and a long tail.

seal

A **seal** is a large sea animal with gray fur and whiskers. Seals have flippers that help them swim.

season

spring

summer

fall

winter

A **season** is a time of year. There are four seasons and they always follow the same order: **spring**, **summer**, **fall**, and **winter**.

seat belt

A **seat belt** is a safety strap in a vehicle. You wear a seat belt around your body to hold you in place.

seaweed

Seaweed is a plant that grows in the sea.

seed

A **seed** is the part of a plant that grows into a new plant.

seesaw

A **seesaw** is a balancing toy for two people. They sit at opposite ends of a long plank that goes up and down.

sell

To **sell** something is to give it to someone in return for money.

seven

Seven is the number that comes after six and before eight.

sew

To **sew** is to join material together using a needle and thread.

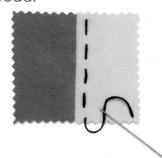

shadow

A **shadow** is a dark shape that you make when you stand in the way of light.

shake

To **shake** something is to move it quickly up and down and from side to side.

shape

A **shape** is the outside line of something. Circles, squares, triangles, and rectangles are all shapes.

share

To **share** something is to give part of it to another person. This boy is sharing his lunch with a friend.

shark

A **shark** is a large sea animal with lots of huge, sharp **teeth.**

sharp

When something is **sharp,** it has an edge or a point that can cut things.

sheep

A **sheep** is a farm animal with a thick, wool coat. A female sheep is called a **ewe** and a male sheep is a **ram.**

shelf

A **shelf** is a long piece of wood that you keep things on.

shell

A **shell** is the hard, outside covering of an egg, nut, or animal.

seashell

ship

A **ship** is a large boat that sails on the sea. Passenger ships carry people.

shirt

A **shirt** is a garment that you wear on the top part of your body.

shoe

A **shoe** is a strong covering for your foot. Shoes protect your **feet.**

shop

When you **shop** you go look at things to buy.

shower

A **shower** is a spray of water that you stand under to wash yourself.

sit

To **sit** is to rest your bottom on a chair or on the **floor.**

short

When something is **short** it is not long.

shut

When something is **shut** it is not open.

six

Six is the number that comes after five and before seven.

shoulder

Your **shoulder** is the part of your body between your neck and arm.

sing

To **sing** is to make music with your voice.

skate

To **skate** is to glide over ice wearing special boots with metal blades called **ice skates.** Roller skates have wheels on them instead of blades.

shout

To **shout** is to call out very loudly.

sink

When something **sinks,** it goes down below the surface of water or another liquid.

skeleton

A **skeleton** is a collection of bones that make a frame to support the rest of a body.

ski

ski

To **ski** is to slide down snow-covered mountains wearing **skis** on your **feet.**

skip

To **skip** is to jump on one leg and then the other. You can also skip over a rope.

skirt

A **skirt** is a garment that hangs down from the **waist.**

sky

The **sky** is above your head where you can see the sun and clouds.

skyscraper

A **skyscraper** is a very tall building that looks as if it is touching the sky.

sled

A **sled** is a vehicle that is used to carry people over the snow.

sleep

To **sleep** is to close your eyes and rest your body and mind. You go to sleep at night or when you are tired.

slice

A **slice** is a thin piece of a larger object.

slide

A **slide** is a kind of toy. You climb to the top of the ladder and slip down a slippery slope.

slow

When something is **slow** it takes a long time. This tortoise moves slowly.

small

When something is **small** it is little and not very big.

smile

A **smile** is what you do with your face to show that you are happy.

snail

A **snail** is an animal with a soft body and a shell on its back.

snake

A **snake** is an animal with a long, thin body, scaly skin, and no legs.

snow

Snow is tiny, white flakes of frozen water. Snow falls from clouds in cold weather.

snowman

A **snowman** is a figure made out of snow.

soap

Soap is something that you use with water to wash things.

soccer

Soccer is a ball game played by two teams of players who kick a ball to score goals.

sock

A **sock** is a piece of clothing for your foot. You wear socks inside shoes.

sofa

A **sofa** is a long, cushioned **seat** with a back and arms. Two or three people can sit on a sofa.

soldier

A **soldier** is a person who is a member of an army.

solid

When something is **solid**, it keeps its shape. This popsicle is solid because it is frozen.

space

Space is the place above the Earth where there is no air. The planets are in space.

spacecraft

A **spacecraft** is a vehicle that travels in space.

space suit

A **space suit** is a special suit worn by astronauts that lets them move freely in space.

sparrow

A **sparrow** is a small, brown bird. Some sparrows sing.

spider

A **spider** is an animal with eight hairy legs. Spiders spin **webs** to catch small insects to eat.

spill

To **spill** something is to knock it out of its container by accident.

spoon

A **spoon** is something that you use to pick up food.

sport

A **sport** is a game or a competition to exercise your body. There are lots of different sports, such as baseball, ice hockey, and running.

square

A **square** is a shape with four corners and four equal sides.

squash

To **squash** something is to press it and make it flat.

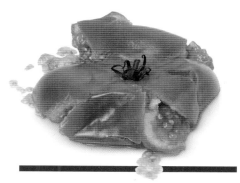

squeeze

To **squeeze** something is to press it. This boy is squeezing the **toothpaste** tube.

squirrel

A **squirrel** is a furry animal with a long, bushy tail. Squirrels live in trees and eat nuts.

stable

A **stable** is a building for horses to live in.

stamp

A **stamp** is a small piece of sticky paper that you put on an envelope. A stamp shows that you have paid to mail a letter.

stand

To **stand** is to be on your **feet** without moving.

star

A **star** is a bright light in space. You can see lots of stars at night.

starfish

A **starfish** is a sea animal with arms that make the shape of a star.

start

To **start** is to begin something. This girl is starting a race.

steering wheel

A **steering wheel** is the part of a car that you hold to turn the wheels.

stem

stem ———

A **stem** is the part of a plant from which the flowers and leaves grow.

stone

A **stone** is a small, hard piece of rock.

stopwatch

A **stopwatch** is a special kind of watch that you use to time a race.

strawberry

A **strawberry** is a red, juicy fruit with bumpy skin.

stream

A **stream** is a small river.

string

String is a strong, thick thread that you use to tie things together.

stripe

A **stripe** is a band of color. All these items have stripes on them.

submarine

A **submarine** is a type of ship that travels underwater.

sugar

Sugar is a sweet food made from **sugarcane**. You use sugar to sweeten other foods.

sugarcane

sun

The **sun** is the huge star that gives the Earth heat and light.

sunglasses

Sunglasses are dark glasses that you wear to protect your eyes from strong sunlight.

supermarket

A **supermarket** is a large shop that sells food and things for the house.

swan

A **swan** is a large water bird with a long neck and webbed **feet.**

swim

To **swim** is to move yourself through water using your arms and legs.

swimming pool

A **swimming pool** is a container filled with water for water play.

swing

A **swing** is a hanging **seat** that you sit on which moves back and forth.

sword

A **sword** is a long, metal blade with a handle at one end.

synagogue

A **synagogue** is a building where Jewish people meet to pray.

tambourine

A **tambourine** is a round musical instrument with metal rings. You shake a tambourine to make a sound.

team

A **team** is a group of people who work or play together.

table

A **table** is a piece of furniture with a flat top and legs.

taxi

A **taxi** is a car with a **driver** you can rent to take you somewhere.

tear

A **tear** is a drop of water that comes out of your eye.

tadpole

A **tadpole** is a tiny animal that lives in water. Tadpoles grow into frogs.

tea

tea leaves

Tea is a drink made from dried plant leaves.

tail

A **tail** is the part of an animal's body that sticks out at the back.

tear

To **tear** something is to pull it apart.

teacher

A **teacher** is a person who helps you learn things.

tall

When something is **tall**, it is higher than usual. The girl on the right is taller than her friend.

telephone

A **telephone** is an instrument for talking to someone who is far away. A **cellphone** is a wireless telephone.

cellphone

telescope

A **telescope** is an instrument that makes faraway objects look bigger and closer.

television

A **television** is a machine that receives messages sent through the air and turns them into sounds and pictures.

temple

A **temple** is a building where people go to pray.

ten

Ten is the number that comes after nine and before eleven.

tennis

Tennis is a game in which two or four players hit a ball with a racket over a net.

tent

A **tent** is a **cloth** shelter you camp in.

theater

A **theater** is a building where you go to see plays, movies, and performances.

thermometer

A **thermometer** is an instrument that measures how hot or cold something is. You can take your **temperature** with a thermometer.

thigh

Your **thigh** is the part of your leg between your hip and your knee.

thin

When something is **thin** it is not fat or thick.

thistle

A **thistle** is a prickly plant with a purple flower.

thorn

A **thorn** is a sharp point on the stem of some plants.

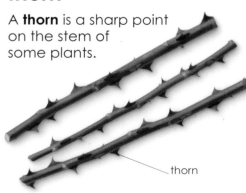

thorn

thread

A **thread** is a thin string used for sewing.

79

three

Three is the number that comes after two and before four.

thumb

Your **thumb** is the thick, short finger nearest to your wrist.

ticket

A **ticket** is a piece of paper that shows you have paid, or have to pay, for something.

tie

A **tie** is a narrow strip of material that is tied around a shirt collar.

tie

To **tie** something is to knot it together.

tiger

A **tiger** is a big, wild cat with orange and black stripes.

tile

A **tile** is a thin, flat covering for **walls** and **floors**.

time

Time is a measurement in **hours**, **minutes**, and **seconds**.

tiptoe

To **tiptoe** is to walk on your toes as quietly as you can.

tired

When you feel **tired**, you need to rest or sleep.

toad

A **toad** is an animal that looks like a big frog with a rough skin.

toboggan

A **toboggan** is a flat-bottomed sled that is curved up at the front. You slide down snowy slopes on a toboggan.

toe

Your **toe** is one of the five digits on the end of your foot.

toilet

A **toilet** is what you sit on to get rid of the waste in your body.

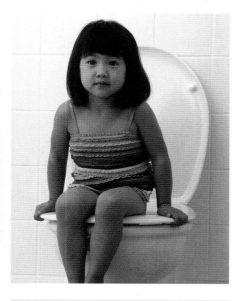

tomato

A **tomato** is a round, red fruit that you eat in salads.

tongue

Your **tongue** is the long, soft muscle inside your mouth. You can lick things with your tongue.

tool

A **tool** is something that helps you do a job. Hammers, pliers, screwdrivers, and wrenches are all tools.

tooth

Your **tooth** is one of the hard, white bones in your mouth. You bite and chew with your **teeth.**

toothbrush

A **toothbrush** is a small brush that you use to clean your **teeth.** You put **toothpaste** on a toothbrush.

top

The **top** of something is the highest part of it. This boy is at the top of the slide.

tornado

A **tornado** is a very strong wind that whirls around and around. Tornados can rip up trees and knock down houses.

toucan

A **toucan** is a black-and-white bird with a large, brightly colored beak.

tourist

A **tourist** is a person who visits places of interest.

towel

A **towel** is a piece of **cloth** you use to dry yourself.

town

A **town** is a place with lots of houses, stores, and schools where people live and work.

toy

A **toy** is something to play with.

tractor

A **tractor** is a farm machine that is used to pull heavy machinery.

traffic

Traffic is all the cars, buses, motorcycles, and other vehicles that travel on the road.

train

A **train** is a line of railroad cars that are pulled along a track by an engine. Trains carry people and things from one place to another.

transparent

When something is **transparent**, it is clear, so you can see through it. This glass is transparent.

trapeze

A **trapeze** is a type of swing that is used by acrobats.

tray

A **tray** is a flat surface with handles that you use to carry food and drinks.

treasure

Treasure is gold, silver, coins, jewels, and other precious things. A treasure chest is a box where you keep valuable objects.

tree

A **tree** is a large plant with leaves, branches, and a thick **trunk**.

triangle

A **triangle** is a shape with three straight sides and three corners.

trick

A **trick** is an amazing thing you can do to surprise people. This boy is pulling cards out of a hat.

tricycle

A **tricycle** is a riding toy with three wheels.

trophy

A **trophy** is a large, metal cup that may be given as a prize.

truck

A **truck** is a big, powerful vehicle that is used to carry heavy loads. This truck has an open back for tipping out its load.

trumpet

A **trumpet** is a musical instrument that is made out of brass. You blow into the mouthpiece and press the **valves** to make a sound.

valve

trunk

A **trunk** is an elephant's long nose. Elephants use their trunks to breathe, squirt water into their mouths, and to pick up things.

T-shirt

A **T-shirt** is a collarless shirt with short sleeves.

tuba

A **tuba** is a large, brass instrument with a wide bell. It produces deep, full tones.

tugboat

A **tugboat** is a small, very powerful boat that is used to pull bigger boats in and out of harbor.

tugboat

tulip

A **tulip** is a cup-shaped flower that grows from a bulb and blooms in the spring.

tunnel

A **tunnel** is a long passage cut through a hill or under the ground.

turkey

A **turkey** is a large farm bird with black-and-white feathers and a long, red chin.

turtle

A **turtle** is an animal with a scaly body covered by a hard shell. Turtles live on land and in water.

tusk

Tusks are the long, pointed **teeth** that some animals have. This elephant has two tusks.

tusk

twig

A **twig** is a small, thin branch of a tree. Leaves grow on twigs.

twin

A **twin** is one of two **children** that were born at the same time to the same parents.

two

Two is the number that comes after one and before three.

umbrella

An **umbrella** is a canopy of cloth on a metal frame. An umbrella keeps you dry when it rains.

under

To be **under** something is to be below it. The toy soldier is standing under the arch.

underwear

Underwear is clothing that you wear under other clothes. Underpants and undershirts are underwear.

undress

To **undress** is to take off your clothes. You undress to get ready for bed.

unicorn

A **unicorn** is an imaginary animal. It looks like a horse with a long, twisted horn on its **forehead.**

university

A **university** is a place where you can go to learn after finishing high school.

up

When something goes **up** it moves to a higher place. This ball is up in the air.

V v

vacuum cleaner

A **vacuum cleaner** is a machine that sucks up dirt from the floor.

valley

A **valley** is the low land between two hills.

vase

A **vase** is a container for holding cut flowers.

vegetable

A **vegetable** is a plant with roots or leaves that you can eat either cooked or raw. There are lots of different kinds of vegetables.

vehicle

A **vehicle** is a machine that carries people and things from one place to another. Cars, buses, and trucks are all vehicles.

veterinarian

A **veterinarian** (or vet for short) is a type of doctor who cares for animals when they are sick or injured.

village

A **village** is a small group of houses and shops in the countryside.

vine

A **vine** is a climbing plant. Grapes grow on vines in fields called **vineyards.**

vinegar

Vinegar is a sour liquid that is used to flavor or preserve food. It is formed when wine, cider, or beer ferments.

violin

A **violin** is a musical instrument made out of wood. You hold it under your chin and draw a **bow** across its strings.

bow

volcano

A **volcano** is a mountain with a hole in the top. Sometimes hot melted rocks, gas, and ash burst out of a volcano.

vulture

A **vulture** is a large bird with a bald head. Vultures eat dead animals.

Ww

wagon

A **wagon** is a cart that is used to carry heavy loads. Wagons are sometimes pulled by horses.

waiter

A **waiter** is a person who serves food in a restaurant.

walk

To **walk** is to move by using your legs and **feet.**

walking stick

A **walking stick** is a long, thin piece of wood that you use to help you walk.

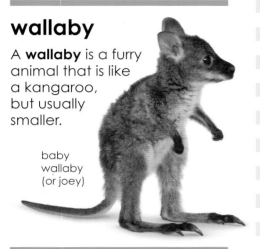

wallaby

A **wallaby** is a furry animal that is like a kangaroo, but usually smaller.

baby wallaby (or joey)

wallet

A **wallet** is a small, flat case that you keep your money in.

walrus

A **walrus** is a big sea animal with a large body and two long, curved tusks.

wash

To **wash** is to clean yourself with soap and water.

watch

To **watch** something is to look at it carefully.

watch

A **watch** is a small clock that you wear on your wrist.

water

Water is the clear liquid that comes out of a faucet. Water falls from the sky as rain.

waterfall

A **waterfall** is a stream or river flowing over the edge of a rock.

water lily

A **water lily** is a flower that grows on ponds and lakes.

watermelon

A **watermelon** is a large fruit with a red or yellow watery inside.

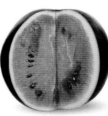

wave

To **wave** is to move your hand to say hello or good-bye.

wear

To **wear** something is to put it on. These girls are wearing hats on their heads, glasses over their eyes, and clothes on their bodies.

wedding

A **wedding** is a special occasion when two people get married.

week

A **week** is seven days long. There are 52 weeks in a year.

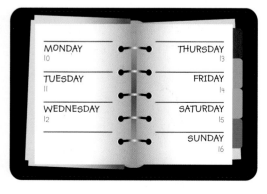

weigh

To **weigh** something is to find out how heavy it is.

wet

When something is **wet**, it is covered with water. This dog is wet and is shaking himself dry.

whale

A **whale** is a huge sea animal that breathes air. Whales are the largest living animals.

wheat

Wheat is a plant that we grind to make flour and other foods.

wheel

A **wheel** is a round frame that turns on a rod in order to move things.

wheelbarrow

A **wheelbarrow** is a small cart with a wheel at the front. It can be used to move things, such as sand and **soil**.

wheelchair

A **wheelchair** is a special chair that helps you move around if you can't walk.

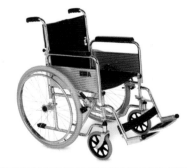

whisker

Whiskers are the long hairs that grow on an animal's face.

whisper

To **whisper** is to talk very quietly so that only one person can hear you.

whistle

A **whistle** is an instrument that makes a sharp, loud sound when you blow it.

white

White is a color. Snow and salt are white.

wide

When something is **wide** it measures a lot from one side to the other.

wind

The **wind** is air that is moving quickly.

windmill

sail

A **windmill** is a machine with sails that turn in the wind and create power. Windmills were used to grind grain into flour.

window

A **window** is an opening in a **wall** that is filled with glass. Windows let in light and air.

wing

Wings are the part of an animal that help it fly.

wing

wire

Wire is a thin, metal thread that is often covered with plastic.

witch

A **witch** is an imaginary woman with magical powers.

wizard

A **wizard** is an imaginary man with magical powers.

wolf

A **wolf** is a wild animal that looks like a large dog.

woman

A **woman** is a grown-up girl.

wood

Wood is the hard part of a tree that is used to make tables and chairs.

wool

Wool is the soft, curly hair of a sheep. Wool is spun into yarn and used for knitting or making **cloth.**

world

The **world** is the Earth and everything that lives on it.

worm

A **worm** is a long animal that lives in the ground.

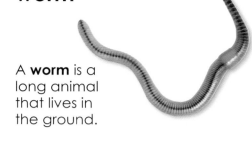

wrinkle

A **wrinkle** is a crease. This dog has wrinkles in his skin.

wrist

Your **wrist** is the joint between your hand and your arm.

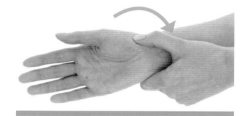

write

To **write** is to put words on paper so that people can read them.

Xx

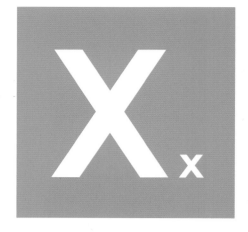

X-ray

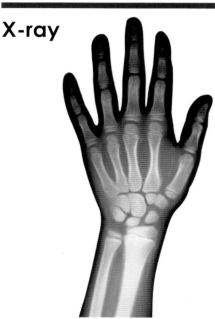

An **X-ray** is a special photograph of the inside of your body. Doctors can look at X-rays to find out if you are sick or injured.

xylophone

A **xylophone** is a musical instrument that is made of metal or wooden bars. You hit the bars with mallets to make musical sounds.

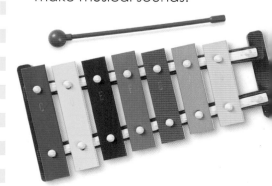

Yy

yacht

A **yacht** is a big, fast boat with a cabin.

yawn

To **yawn** is to open your mouth wide and breathe in deeply. You yawn when you are tired or bored.

year

A **year** is a measure of time that lasts 12 months, 52 weeks, or 365 days.

yellow

Yellow is a color. Lemons and bananas are yellow.

yogurt

Yogurt is a thick, creamy food made from milk. Yogurt often has fruit in it.

yolk

A **yolk** is the yellow part of an egg.

young

A **young** person is someone who is only a few years old. This baby is young.

Zz

zebra

A **zebra** is an animal that looks like a horse with black-and-white stripes on its body.

zero

Zero is the number that comes before one. Zero means nothing.

zipper

A **zipper** holds clothes together.

zoo

A **zoo** is a place where wild animals are kept for people to visit and learn about.

Dictionary games

See if you can solve all these word puzzles, using your dictionary to help you. At the same time, you can practice looking up words and spellings. You will find all the answers to the puzzles somewhere in the dictionary. The pictures will help you find the word you are looking for more easily.

Every puzzle has a special box where the first question is answered for you, so you can see what to do. Remember to write your answers down on a piece of paper, not in this book! You can play most of the games by yourself, but sometimes you will need a friend to help you. Have fun!

Animal alphabet

These animals should be in alphabetical order, but they have gotten all mixed up. Use the alphabet at the top of this page to put them back in order.

armadillo

tiger

rabbit

vulture

pelican

elephant

dinosaur

Spelling puzzle

You probably know the names of the things pictured below, but can you spell them? Try alone first, and then use your dictionary to see how many you got right.

acrobat

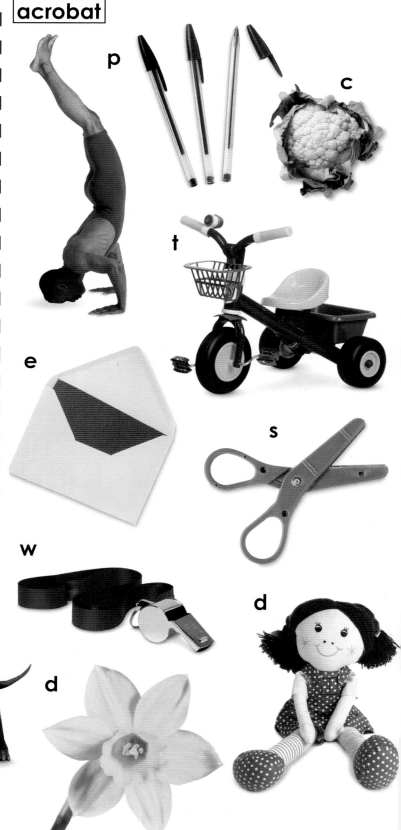

p

c

t

e

s

w

d

d

92

Word detective

Find the right word to answer these questions. You can use the clues to help you, just like a detective does.

> • What do you call a person who breaks into a building to steal something?
> The word begins with the letter **b**.
>
> ## burglar

• What is the name for precious things like gold, silver, coins, and jewels?
Look for the things that sparkle on page 82.

• What can you wear over your face to disguise yourself?
Find the hidden face under **m**.

• What do you call a person who protects people and makes sure laws are obeyed?
Look for a word beginning with **p**.

• What do you wear on your feet to protect them?
Try page 71.

Dictionary lucky dip

This is a game that you can play by yourself or with a friend.

1) Think of a letter of the alphabet.

2) Now, close your dictionary and try to open it again at exactly the right place to find the letter you have chosen.

You score two points if you find the correct page, and one point if you are close.

Test your memory

Look carefully at all the objects below for one minute. Next close the dictionary and see how many things you can remember. Write them down, and then try arranging the words in alphabetical order to make your own little dictionary.

Which one doesn't belong?

If you look carefully at the things below, you will see that in each group there is one which "doesn't belong." Can you figure out which one it is by reading the dictionary definitions?

snake   **beetle**   **bee**

The **snake** is the one that doesn't belong because it is not an insect.

crown   **glove**   **hat**

grapes   **pear**   **carrots**

trumpet   **recorder**   **violin**

▌ Find that word

Use the index at the back of this book to help you answer these questions. Look for each word in **bold** type in the index, and it will tell you the page number you want.

> • What is **indigo?**
> Indigo is one of the seven colors of a rainbow.

• Who do **guide dogs** help?

• What is a **stallion?**

• How do **firefighters** travel to a fire?

• Why do people send out **invitations?**

• Is there another word for a **rain forest?**

• **Mars** is a planet. Can you name any others?

Sound-alikes

Some words sound the same when you say them, but they have different meanings. With a friend, say these words out loud, and then take turns looking up the meanings. Do you know more pairs of words like this?

bat	**bat**
A **bat** is a kind of stick that is used to hit a ball.	A **bat** is a small, furry animal with wings.

flour   **flower**

nut   **nut**

orange   **orange**

pair   **pear**

right   **write**

scale   **scale**

tie   **tie**

Animal jumble

Here are lots of animals that are all jumbled up.
Answer the questions to find out which animals
make pairs or sets. Remember that the dictionary
definitions will help you.

Which of these birds cannot fly?

toucan

jaguar

sheep

dolphin

goose

cat

crab

lamb

dog

gosling

penguin

Can you find four baby animals?

How many of these birds can swim?

ostrich

Which of these animals live in, or around, water?

starfish

kitten

There are three cats on this page. Can you point to them?

puppy

crocodile

Index of additional words

Actor 4
Africa 19
afternoon 22
Antarctica 19
antler 22, 49
April 49
Asia 19
August 49
aunt 19
Australia 19
Baker 6
bakery 6
bathroom 8
bedroom 8
bike 9
billy 33
boar 59
bolt 52
bow 86
bridegroom 11
brother 28
build 12
builder 12
bull 20
bus stop 12
Calf 20
calves 20
campsite 14
cattle 20
CD (compact disc) 19
ceiling 67
cellphone 78
chest of drawers 24
chick 16
children 16, 58, 84
cloth 18, 19, 29, 40, 59, 79, 82, 90
coffee beans 18

compact disc player 19
copper 48
Daughter 56
December 49
digital 29
diver 23
doe 22
drake 25
driver 12, 25, 78
drumstick 25
duckling 25
Emerald 40
entrance 27
Europe 19
evening 22
ewe 71
eyebrow 28
Fall 70
farmer 28
father 28
fawn 22
February 49
feet 9, 25, 30, 37, 41, 71, 73, 76, 77, 86
female 33
firefighter 29
fishing net 51
floor 67, 72, 80
foal 37
football 31
forehead 28, 85
France 19
Friday 88
Gander 34
geese 34
gosling 34
grandchildren 34
grandfather 34

grandmother 34
guide dog 10
gymnasium 34
Hairbrush 49
halves 35
handlebars 9
hen 16
highway 66
hour 22, 80
husband 11
Ice skate 72
indigo 64
inventor 39
invitation 39
iron 47, 48
January 49
jewelry 33, 40, 57
joey 87
juggler 41
July 49
June 49
Jupiter 59
Keyboard 19
kid 33
Lawnmower 43
letter 27
lioness 45
Magician 46
male 11
mane 45
March 49
mare 37
Mars 59
May 49
men 4, 58
Mercury 59
mice 50

minute 80
Monday 88
morning 22
mother 28
Nanny 33
Neptune 59
North America 19
North Pole 27
November 49
Oats 15
October 49
Padlock 45
pants 18, 40
parking lot 14
pedal 9
piglet 59
pitcher 40
princess 61
Rail 64
rain forest 41
ram 71
rooster 16
ruby 40
rye 15
sailboat 68
sailor 68
sandcastle 68
Saturday 88
Saturn 59
saxophone 39
screen 19, 50
seashell 71
seat 9, 68, 74, 77
second 80
September 49
sister 28
ski 73

smokestack 16
soil 9, 12, 25, 60, 67, 88
son 56
sorting office 61
South America 19
South Pole 27
sow 59
spring 70
stag 22
stallion 37
steel 47, 48
sugarcane 77
summer 70
Sunday 88
Teeth 4, 9, 40, 44, 69, 71, 81, 84
temperature 79
thunderstorm 45
Thursday 88
toothpaste 75, 81
trunk 11, 83
Tuesday 88
Uncle 19
Uranus 59
Valve 83
Venus 59
vineyard 86
violet 64
Waist 9, 37, 73
wall 67, 80, 89
web 75
Wednesday 88
wife 11
winter 70
women 4, 24, 58

Acknowledgements

Dorling Kindersley would like to thank the following people for their assistance in the production of this book:

Malavika Talukder, Suneha Dutta, Roma Malik, Neha Chaudhary, Pankaj Deo, Rashmi Rajan, Pragati Nagpal, Archana Ramachandran, Suparna Sengupta, Antara Moitra, Jubbi Francis, Mona Joshi, Neha Gupta, Dharini Ganesh, Parameshwari Sircar, Samira Sood.

Picture Credits

The publisher would like to thank the following for their kind permission to reproduce their photographs:
(Key: a-above; b-below/bottom; c-center; f-far; l-left; r-right; t-top)

4 Corbis: Boris Roessler / epa (cra). Fotolia: Eric Isselée (cr). Getty Images: momentimages (bc). 5 Getty Images: David Madison / Photodisc (cl). 6 Fotolia: Arto (br). 7 Corbis: Tetra Images (cr). Fotolia: rgbspace (bl). Getty Images: Amy Eckert / Photodisc (cra); Ryan McVay / Photodisc (c). 8 Dorling Kindersley: Duracell Ltd (cl). Fotolia: Nataliya Kashina (bc). Getty Images: Jetta Productions / Iconica (c). 9 Fotolia: iNNOCENt (bl). Getty Images: Fuse (c). 10 Alamy Images: Baby I Got It (tc). 11 Getty Images: Johner / Johner Images (br). 12 Getty Images: Hisham Ibrahim / Photographer's Choice RF (tc). 13 Getty Images: Glow Images (bl). 14 Corbis: John Lund / Marc Romanelli / Blend Images (bc). Dorling Kindersley: Paul Wilkinson (ca). Fotolia: Claude Beaubien (tc). Getty Images: Photolove / Cultura (cr). 15 Dorling Kindersley: Stephen Oliver (br). Getty Images: W. Wisniewski (br). Getty Images: Floresco Productions / OJO Images (tl); ImagesBazaar / the Agency Collection (cra); Monica Vinella / Photonica (cra). 17 Getty Images: Colorblind / Photodisc (clb). 18 Fotolia: Patrick Hermans (ca). 19 Fotolia: design56 (bc). Getty Images: Michael Blann / Photodisc (clb); Yoshikazu Tsuno / AFP (cla). 20 Dreamstime.com: Constantin Bogdan Carstina (bl). Getty Images: Dimitri Vervitsiotis / Digital Vision (cra). 21 Getty Images: Peter Dazeley / Photographer's Choice (c); PM Images / Iconica (tl). 22 Getty Images: Jamie Marshall (c). Fotolia: Vladimir Mucibabic (bl). 23 Getty Images: Matthias Kulka (tl). Fotolia: dinahr (tr). Getty Images: CAP53 / Vetta (ca). 25 Getty Images: Thierry Dosogne / Photodisc (br); Fuse (tl); Roy Ooms / All Canada Photos (cla). 27 Corbis: Raygun / cultura (cb). 28 Getty Images: Randy Faris (bc). 29 Dorling Kindersley: Richard Leeney (c). Getty Images: Ghislain & Marie David de Lossy / Taxi (ca). 31 Getty Images: Ove Eriksson / Nordic Photos (clb); Masanobu Hirose / Sebun Photo / amana images (c). 32 Corbis: Bruce Connolly (cb). 33 Dorling Kindersley: Lindsey Stock Collection (tc); Comstock Images / Alamy (cr); David Cook / blueshiftstudios / Alamy (br). Getty Images: Andrew Olney / Stone (bc). 34 Getty Images: Steve Debenport / the Agency Collection (c). 35 Getty Images: Noel Hendrickson / Digital Vision (cb). 36 Getty Images: Andrew Geiger / Riser (br). 37 Getty Images: Studio Box / Photographer's Choice (br). 39 Corbis: Natalie Tepper / Arcaid (tl). Getty Images: Vincenzo Lombardo / Robert Harding World Imagery (cla); Dieter Spannknebel / Photodisc (tl). 40 Dorling Kindersley: Geoff Brightling / Peter Minister - modelmaker (bc). 41 Corbis: Andreas Kunert (bl); Ashely Jouhar (tl). 42 Getty Images: Christoph Martin / Lifesize (tl); Dahl, Per / Johner Images (ca); David Samuel Robbins / Photographer's Choice (cra). 43 Corbis: Destinations (cr). Getty Images: Robert Glusic (tc); Michael Hitoshi / Digital Vision (cb). 44 Corbis: Tim Pannell (br). Dorling Kindersley: Philip Dowell (tc); Richard Leeney (cra). 45 Fotolia: samott (cr). Getty Images: Peter Arnold / Digital Vision (bl). 46 Dorling Kindersley: Blend Images / PunchStock (bl). 47 Dorling Kindersley: Ryan McVay (bl). Getty Images: Tim Draper (c). Dreamstime.com: Arvind Balaraman (bc). Fotolia: Sandra Gligorjevic (crb). Getty Images: Lucas Lenci Photo / The Image Bank (bl). 48 Getty Images: Christopher Bissell / Stone (tc). 50 Corbis: Dean Conger (br). Getty Images: Buena Vista Images / Photodisc (tc). 51 Fotolia: Alex White (cb). Getty Images: Jack Hollingsworth / Photodisc (bl). 52 Corbis: Tom & Dee Ann McCarthy (ca). Getty Images: Joos Mind / Stone (tr). 53 Corbis: Robbie Jack (br); TWPhoto (tr). Fotolia: leschnyhan (ca). 54 Corbis: John O'Boyle / Star Ledger (c). Getty Images: George Doyle / Stockbyte (cla); Godong / Robert Harding World Imagery (bc). 55 Corbis: Ludovic Maisant / Hemis (crb). Dorling Kindersley: SCPhotos / Dallas and John Heaton / Alamy (br). Getty Images: CSA Plastock / CSA Images (cla). 56 Corbis: Charles Gullung (cr). Dreamstime.com: Alekosa (clb). Getty Images: Noel Hendrickson / Digital Vision (tr); B2M Productions / Digital Vision (tc). 57 Corbis: Steve Hix / Somos Images (tl). Dorling Kindersley: Judith Miller / Sylvie Spectrum (cb); Stephen Oliver (bc). Fotolia: Shawn Hempel (bl). Getty Images: Image Source (cr). 58 Getty Images: David Young-Wolff / Photographer's Choice (clb). 59 Corbis: Ed Boettcher (tc). 60 Getty Images: Mark Mann / Taxi (clb). 61 Getty Images: Billy Hustace / Stone. 62 Getty Images: Per Breiehagen / The Image Bank (bl); Andersen Ross / Digital Vision (clb); Hill Creek Pictures / UpperCut Images. 63 Getty Images: Anderson Ross / Blend Images (cra). Dorling Kindersley: Dennis Welsh / UpperCut Images. 64 Corbis: Jose Fuste Raga (c); Warren Jacobi (cr). Dreamstime.com: Tamara Bauer (clb). Getty Images: Westend61 (tr). 65 Getty Images: Juan Silva / FoodPix (cra). 66 Corbis: Pascal Le Segretain / Sygma (crb). Dorling Kindersley: Gary Ombler (bl, tr). Getty Images: Cameron Davidson / Workbook Stock. 67 Corbis: George Hammerstein (crb). Getty Images: Sophia Vourdoukis / Taxi (cra). 68 Corbis: Denis Scott (cr). Getty Images: Alex Cao / Photodisc (cla); Thinkstock Images / Comstock Images (br). 69 Corbis: Lew Robertson (clb). Dorling Kindersley: Jerry Young (bc). Getty Images: Lenora Gim / Photonica (cra). 70 Corbis: Kazuo Honzawa / Sebun Photo / amanaimages; Randy Faris (bc). Getty Images: Todd Pearson / Photographer's Choice (tc). 71 Corbis: JLP / Jose Pelaez (bc); Jose Luis Pelaez Inc / Blend Images (cla). Getty Images: MoMo Productions / Photonica (tl). 72 Corbis: Bettmann (bc); Norbert Schaefer (bl). Getty Images: Sam Edwards / OJO Images (br). 73 Getty Images: Dan Kenyon / Stone (cb). 74 Dorling Kindersley: Jupiterimages / Alamy (cr); Bob Gathany (br); Stephen Oliver (tr). Getty Images: Robert Llewellyn / Workbook Stock (crb); Ryan McVay / Photodisc (cb). 76 Dorling Kindersley: Judith Miller / Freeman's (tl). Dorling Kindersley: Grain Belt Pictures / Alamy (cb). Getty Images: Taylor S. Kennedy / National Geographic (tr). 78 Dorling Kindersley: Paul Wilkinson (br); Judith Miller / Lyon and Turnbull Ltd. (tl). Fotolia: AVAVA (bc); Mykola Velychko (tr). Getty Images: a.collectionRF (crb); Hisham Ibrahim / Photographer's Choice RF (ca). 79 Corbis: Owaki - Kulla (cb). Dorling Kindersley: Stephen Oliver (cra). Getty Images: Yasuhide Fumoto / Digital Vision (cla). 80 Dreamstime.com: Eslivanova (bc). 81 Getty Images: PhotoAlto / Sandro Di Carlo Darsa (bc); Chris Stein / Digital Vision (bl). 82 Fotolia: Brandi Engel (clb). Getty Images: Simon Bruty / Photodisc (tr). 83 Dreamstime.com: Glenda Powers (cl). Getty Images: Travelpix Ltd / Stone (tl). 84 Dorling Kindersley: Stephen Oliver (bc). Fotolia: Sergey Mostovoy (tl). 86 Corbis: Jim Sugar. 88 Corbis: Benelux (c). Dreamstime.com: Emma Firth (bc); Stockbyte / Photolibrary (cr). 90 Corbis: Yoav Levy / MedNet (cr). 91 Fotolia: GRod (ca). Getty Images: Tony Arruza / Stone (br).

Jacket Credits

Front: Alamy: Melba Photo Agency

All other images © Dorling Kindersley
For further information see: www.dkimages.com